On Giant Shoulders

The history, role, and influence of the *evangelist* in the movement called Methodism.

Robert G. Tuttle, Jr.

Discipleship Resources   **Nashville**

ISBN: 0-88177-006-X

Library of Congress Card Catalog Number: 83-51101

To Lawrence and Mildred Lacour,
whose giant shoulders have launched
many an evangelist, including myself.

Contents

Acknowledgments

Although the primary dedication for this book lists my long-time good friends Larry and Millie Lacour, several others need to be acknowledged as well. The entire project was first the brainchild of Charles Whittle, senior pastor of First United Methodist Church, Abilene, Texas. He not only solicited and inspired my interest, he suggested a publisher as well. From the beginning, Chester Custer, executive director for Discipleship Resources, has provided careful direction, guiding me toward a completed manuscript that will hopefully benefit not only the evangelists but the church-at-large. To both these men I say thank you sincerely.

Mention must also be made of Oral Roberts University Provost & Vice-President for Academic Affairs Carl Hamilton, and Vice-Provost for Theological and Spiritual Affairs and Dean of the School of Theology Jim Buskirk. They encouraged me greatly, making available the word processing center for both writing and editing. I am in their debt. I must also acknowledge the particular efforts of Arlene Dewell whose hard work enabled me to press on toward completion.

Finally, deep appreciation to my wife Artie and our children Sarajane, Bill, Marilee, Eric, and Elizabeth. God bless them one and all.

Introduction

Recently a friend of mine attempted to take his own life. I rushed him to the hospital. Watching his body struggle for life that the mind no longer wanted captured my full attention. I shall never forget it. Life in the balance puts things in perspective. Why do we listen carefully to the words of the dying? Their final gasps demand our full attention. We strain as if seeking the key to some unlocked treasure. Jesus wisely waited until the eve of the crucifixion to speak at length of the work of the Holy Spirit. That guaranteed an audience. In the past few weeks, my father has suffered a heart attack and I, myself, have had symptoms which could have suggested (though the tests proved negative) a life-threatening disease. Things have had greater focus. Ordinary events have stood out in sharp relief. As I pondered all of this, suddenly it hit me! That is the role of the evangelist. Let me explain.

The evangelists so dramatize the battle—the conflict between good and evil, light and darkness—that our very lives seem to pass before our eyes. The sheer urgency of their message captures us, if but for a moment. We are reminded (to use the words of John Wesley): "I am a creature of a day, passing through life as an arrow through the air . . . till, a few moments hence, I am no more seen; I drop into an unchangeable eternity!" (John Wesley, *Works*, 3rd ed., vol. IV, p. 3). Everyone is terminal. If we are to win this battle that we wage—this battle against time and meaninglessness—if death is to become a door to the Eternal, then we must conquer life, however brief. Life itself is the prize—eternal life, abundant life. The evangelists tell us that in order to conquer life we must have help—God's help. Ephesians 2:4-5 reads: "But because of His great love for us, God, who is rich in mercy, made us alive with Christ even when we were dead in transgressions— it is by grace you have been saved." The evangelists are the voices crying in the wilderness, the ministers of city and hamlet, the preachers on radio and television, the prophets of warning and promise who so demonstrate the power of the gospel that people, as if some Philippian jailer shaking in the midst of an earthquake, cry out (in one form or another): "What must I do to be saved" (Acts 16:30). As with Paul and Silas, the answer is still the same: "Believe in the Lord Jesus . . ." (Acts 16:31). It is primarily to these evangelists that this book is dedicated—not that they need such a book. I simply welcome the opportunity to say thank you on behalf of United Methodism for a job well done. May your tribe increase.

Although I was more or less "drafted" to write this book, once the research was begun the assignment became an obsession. I have discovered what I had long suspected: that United Methodism, perhaps more than any other movement, owes its very existence to the role and influence of the evangelist. The historical significance is not simply a record of past glory but lends weight to the present importance of those called to proclaim the gospel as United Methodist evangelists. Ask for a show of hands in almost any United Methodist gathering as to those who first responded to the claims of the gospel upon their lives in some kind of an evangelistic meeting. The results might well surprise you. Again, as The United Methodist Church looks to the future, I welcome this opportunity to remind her of such an important legacy. I pray that this does it justice.

As for the outline of the book itself, I have decided on several different tacks focusing in four major areas and time frames. *First*, we must start at the beginning. The story of the evangelist in Methodism is as old as its name. John Wesley was an evangelist extraordinaire. His journal account of the eighteenth century Evangelical Revival is a carefully documented record of thousands upon thousands who responded to the call and nurture of the Methodist evangelist, both lay and clergy. The whole of the United Kingdom was alive with itinerant preachers spreading scriptural holiness throughout the land.

Second, although vastly different in setting and circumstance, the American scene tells a similar story with regard to the impact of the Methodist evangelist. Tireless, self-sacrificing (life expectancy was but 34), totally committed to Christ and church, they answered the call to city and frontier alike. When the weather and conditions seemed impassable, the early Americans joked: "Nothin' out tonight but crows and Methodist preachers." Except it was no joke. It was fact. Francis Asbury preached fewer sermons but traveled more miles than John Wesley himself. Like Wesley, his journal accounts of early Methodism document time and again the faithfulness of those "trampling out the vineyards." First along the eastern seaboard but then across the Appalachians, the Methodist evangelist, armed with the Word of God, fired by the Holy Spirit, compelled by the Great Commandment, and driven by the Great Commission, made Methodism, more than any other, the religion of America.

Third, lest we forget our roots within *United* Methodism, it is absolutely essential to include the influence of the evangelists within the United Brethren and the Evangelical Association. Both Otterbein and Albright labored as evangelists among the German-speaking communities of the fledgling republic. Our connection is solid from the beginning. Otterbein was present at Asbury's ordination and Albright attended a Methodist class meeting for some months following his conversion. Although Otterbein had reformed roots, the United Brethren, as well as the Evangelical Association, quickly became compatible both with Arminian theology and Methodist polity. Otterbein and Albright bring something in style and technique that is valuable and unique to our study as a whole. Their plea for unity sounded an alarm which should have been carefully heeded. It was not. *United* Methodism could be a memorial to their peculiar genius as evangelists of vision and power. They would certainly have accepted the invitation of John Wesley: "If your heart is as my heart, then give me your hand."

Fourth, the story of the United Methodist evangelist on the contemporary scene is both discouraging and encouraging. For a time the appointment as evangelist was the first step out of the connectional system. Preachers were sometimes "located" as evangelists as a disciplinary precaution to further trouble within the local body. Fortunately, in more recent years this image has changed considerably. Persons such as E. Stanley Jones traveled the world as Methodist evangelists. His obvious gifts set a new tone for the twentieth and twenty-first centuries. Far ahead of his time in his sensitivity to a renewed emphasis on the person and work of the Holy Spirit, Stanley Jones created a powerful precedent for all of us today. If one goes back far enough, the past as well as the future is bright. I believe that God is at this moment raising up a new breed of United Methodist evangelists who are better equipped with the tools for ministry than any before them. We can all pray that The United Methodist Church as a whole is still open to their message of repentance and faith.

Another tack (actually a tack within a tack) employed in our outline is to begin each major part with a model. This model is not to say that this is the way it must be done. Far from it! The model presented is simply a reminder of what God can do through the lives of those totally committed to a worthy call. Wesley, Asbury, Otterbein, Albright, and Jones were all evangelists effective in their own time and in their own way. We follow them as they followed Jesus, but no further. Following the model for each period, I have gathered material which I believe best tells the story of the history, role, and influence of the evangelist within that particular period.

Having said all of this, allow me to prepare you for Chapter One with a brief word of exhortation. Too frequently the evangelist (especially the traveling evangelist) leads a lonely life, sometimes by necessity, sometimes by choice. Some are too easily intimidated by the system. They stand somewhat aloof. To those I say, do not do it. Get in touch with your roots. Be proud. You stand on giant shoulders. Your ministry is needed (if not entirely appreciated) if our great church is to embrace the challenge of an uncertain future.

Part I
The Evangelical Revival

Chapter 1: The John Wesley Model

His friends and followers have no reason to be ashamed of the name of *Methodist* . . .

John Whitehead

Let me take you back over 200 years to an inn located in a small but busy English town. Picture a large room dimly lit by candlelight. Two men sit arguing at a table over several pints of beer. One begins to curse the other, bitterly invoking the name of God. Just then a small man enters by a side door and after observing the two in heated debate sighs almost painfully. His look is not one of judgment or anger but apparent disappointment. As the two struggle to rise as if leaving, the man watching approaches the one who had been cursing: "Sir, my name is Wesley. Do you see that door over there? When you leave, be certain to look both ways as you step into the street. Please do not let a horse or carriage run over you. If you were to die with that blasphemy on your head you would surely find the hottest place in the lake of fire."

That story was told to me in good faith. Quite frankly, I cannot find a reference for it, although John Wesley was certainly capable of such candor. Perhaps there is not much gospel evident there, but Wesley was such a man and if the story is true, I would be willing to wager that God was somehow at work.

Samuel Johnson once stated: "I hate to meet John Wesley; the dog enchants with his conversation and then breaks away to go and visit some old woman." Proof again that one man's dog is another man's disciple. That was the spirit of the evangelist, John Wesley. He was always dashing off to visit some old woman or, even worse, to speak a timely word to a drunken blasphemer about to step blindly into a busy street.

We know with reasonable certainty that John Wesley's first convert to justification by faith in Jesus Christ was a condemned felon. Even before Wesley's own evangelical conversion, Peter Böhler had insisted that he preach faith until he had faith; and then, because he had faith he would preach it. Within days Wesley's journal entry reads:

1

Accordingly I began preaching this new doctrine, though my soul started back from the work. The first person to whom I offered salvation by faith alone was a prisoner under sentence of death. His name was Clifford.[1]

Listen now to the results of this encounter recorded a few days later.

Mr. Kinchin went with me to the castle, where, after reading prayers, and preaching on "It is appointed unto men once to die," we prayed with the condemned man, first in several forms of prayer, and then in such words as were given us in that hour. He kneeled down in much heaviness and confusion, having "no rest in" his "bones, by reason" of his "sins." After a space he rose up, and eagerly said, "I am now ready to die. I know Christ has taken away my sins; and there is no more condemnation for me." The same composed cheerfulness he showed when he was carried to execution; and in his last moments he was the same, enjoying a perfect peace, in confidence that he was "accepted in the Beloved."[2]

There is irony here. Wesley began to realize his gift as evangelist even before his own experience of faith. A condemned felon on his way to the gallows was brought to the very thing that Wesley wanted most, a certain peace with God, and assurance of acceptance as a child of God. This was soon followed by the well-known experience at Aldersgate. With the world as his parish, Wesley preached the gospel of Jesus Christ, averaging two or three sermons a day for the next fifty-three years. Frequently before the heads of his strongest critics had left their downy pillows, Wesley had served communion, preached two sermons, and ridden thirty miles. So, the model for the evangelist for the Evangelical Revival out of which Methodism sprang to life is an obvious choice. Before moving on, however, let me say a word about the importance of modeling.

Jesus was the master at "show and tell." He modeled what he taught. He ministered so well that his disciples asked: "Teach us to minister." Since that time men and women have served as models for their own day. The Spirit of Jesus Christ remains among us and occasionally surfaces in an extraordinary way. The Evangel, himself, has so captured the minds of some that they demonstrate just what can be accomplished through willing (and sometimes not so willing) obedience to the God of us all. Not that we should attempt to become who they were. God forbid. God calls all of us to be ourselves and in our own way

2

to be faithful to our unique callings. No one else's theory or method can be nearly as effective as our own in our own sphere of influence. We follow others as they follow Jesus—but no further. Nonetheless, these precedents for greatness provide a challenge for today. As suggested in the introduction, the various models serving as the opening chapters for each of the major parts should not imply that this is how it must be done. We can already see a great deal of diversity within this small selection. What these models teach us is just how they succeeded in obeying their evangelistic calls. Again, the precedents here are not only in style and technique but in matters of character and conscience as well. So the outline for each of the modeling chapters seeks to cover a wide spectrum dealing with *message, character, style, motivation,* and finally, *the relevance* of all of this *for today.* Let's get back to John Wesley.

Message. John Wesley's *Works* have been the happy hunting ground for many a preacher seeking to document almost any point of view. Summarizing the basic content of Wesley's message might seem an awesome task. Nonetheless, I believe that it can be done. Not that Wesley was not an enormously complex man. In many ways he was. Furthermore, his theology found focus in attempts to solve problems, not establish doctrine. That is the difference between a practical and a systematic theologian. Yet, in many ways, Wesley was utterly predictable. One day in his diary can be exchanged with almost any other for over fifty years. Also, several recurring themes give us a fairly good feel for the direction in which he was headed. No one could accuse Wesley of concealing what he thought most important. We know where his passion lay. Let's now discuss the general thrust of his message.

Although Wesley was not a systematic theologian, the basic content of his message can be described with reasonable clarity from the study of his published sermons, tracts, treatises, and correspondence. Wesley's message in essence, so akin to the Reformation, affirms God's sovereign will to reverse our "sinful, devilish nature," by the work of the Holy Spirit, a process Wesley called prevenient, justifying, and sanctifying grace (grace being nearly synonymous with the work of the Holy Spirit).

Prevenient or preventing grace, for Wesley, describes the universal work of the Holy Spirit in the hearts and lives of people between conception and conversion. Original sin, according to Wesley, makes it necessary for the Holy Spirit to *initiate* the relationship between God and people. Bound by sin and death, people experience the gentle wooing of the Holy Spirit which prevents them from moving so far from "the way" that when they finally understand the claims of the gospel upon their lives, the Holy Spirit guarantees their freedom to say yes. This understanding of grace constitutes the heart of Wesley's Arminianism and assures the integrity of an evangelistic appeal. Since any appeal calls for response, it is obviously important to be able to make such a response. Grace (prevenient grace) through faith, therefore, established for Wesley the core of the gospel message. His sermons entitled "Salvation by Faith" and "Justification by Faith" set the stage.

Wesley tells us that he preached basically three kinds of sermons. To the unawakened (those not yet convicted of sin), he spoke mainly of death and hell. To those awakened (not yet converted), he spoke mainly of faith. To those converted, he spoke mainly of perfection or entire sanctification. Let's, for a moment, focus at the point of his evangelistic appeal—to those awakened. Faith is the key. Wesley goes to great lengths to define it. He tells us what it is not. It is not that faith of a heathen, or of a devil, or even that of the apostles while Christ remained in the flesh.[3] He tells us what it is. It is, in a general sense, "a divine, supernatural, *evidence* or *conviction*, 'of things not seen,' not discoverable by our bodily senses, as being either past, future, or spiritual. Justifying faith implies, not only a divine evidence or conviction that 'God was in Christ, reconciling the world unto himself;' but a sure trust and confidence that Christ died for *my* sins, that He loved *me* and gave himself for *me*."[4] Then the passage following this statement provides a further key. There he speaks of *repentance*.[5] Wesley's evangelistic thrust insisted that faith build upon a firm foundation. The repentance that led to faith was for Wesley what I sometimes refer to as the "I give up." Let me explain.

It is my conviction that Wesley's "instantaneous" conversion experience took thirteen years to manifest itself fully. The reason for the delay was that it took considerable effort to divest himself of the bankruptcy of his own works-righteousness. Even before leaving for Georgia, Wesley sensed that something was amiss. At that point he attempted to exchange the outward works of "visiting the sick or clothing the naked" for the inward works of a pursuit of holiness "or a union of a soul with God." He comments later that "in this refined way of trusting to my own works and my own righteousness (so zealously inculcated by the mystic writers), I dragged on heavily, finding no comfort or help therein."[6] At long last Wesley resolved to seek salvation through faith by first of all "absolutely renouncing all dependence in whole or in part, upon *my own* works or righteousness; on which I

4

had really grounded my hope of salvation, though I knew it not, from my youth up." [7] This was the point at which Wesley "gave up." His besetting sin was a misplaced trust. He repented. He gave up his faith in his own self-righteousness and determined to trust Christ alone as his sole "justification, sanctification, and redemption." Aldersgate followed shortly thereafter.

For the rest of his life, this "I give up," this (to use the words of à Kempis) "following naked the naked Jesus" became the spearhead for his evangelistic appeal. His watchwords included such warnings as: Do not trust that broken reed of your infant baptism. Do not trust anyone or anything else for salvation apart from Christ. He writes: "As 'there is no other name given under heaven' than that of Jesus of Nazareth, no other merit whereby a condemned sinner can ever be saved from the guilt of sin; so there is no other way of obtaining a share in his merit, than *by faith in His name*." [8] This should provide a key for our understanding of evangelism as well. Again, give it up! Trust Christ alone! God's grace is available to everyone who believes.

In addition, any reference to the Wesleyan message that does not include reference to perfection as the hallmark of Methodism is sadly amiss. Grace continues to work in us throughout our lives.

Sanctifying grace describes the work of the Holy Spirit in the lives of believers between conversion and death. Faith in Christ saves us *from* hell and sin *for* heaven and good works. Imputed righteousness according to Wesley *entitles* one to heaven; imparted righteousness *qualifies* one for heaven. It is here that Wesley goes to great lengths to describe his views on perfection.

The process of sanctification or perfection culminates in an experience of "pure love" as one progresses to the place where love becomes devoid of self-interest. This second work of grace is described as the one purpose of all religion. If one is not perfected in love, one is not "ripe for glory." It is important, however, to note that this perfection was not static but dynamic, always improvable. Neither was it angelic or Adamic. Adam's perfection was objective and absolute while Wesley's perfection was subjective and relative, involving for the most part, intention and motive.

Although Wesley talks about an instantaneous experience called "entire sanctification" subsequent to justification, his major emphasis was the continuous process of going on to perfection. Perhaps first learned from the early church fathers like Macarius and Ephraem Syrus, this emphasis upon continuous process was enforced by Wesley to prevent the horrible expectation of backsliding. Wesley soon learned that the only way to keep Methodists alive was to keep them moving. The same concept of continuous process was later polished by the influence of mystics such as François Fénelon, whose phrase *"moi progressus ad infinitum"* (my progress is without end), greatly impressed Wesley and became a major tool for the perpetuation of the Evangelical Revival. The watchword for the revival became: "Go on to perfection: otherwise you cannot keep what you have."

To conclude this section on the message, it occurs to me that most of us do theology by the way we view people. Wesley viewed people as lost to sin, susceptible to change, vulnerable to defeat, and called to a life of holiness. His message, therefore, was that the Father can forgive, the Son can bring a new life, and the Spirit can wholly sanctify. John Wesley not only preached and taught this message, he tried to live it as well.

Character. Some research has been done on the effects one's character has on one's ability to communicate effectively. Much of what has been done speaks of the importance of congruency. If our ministry is to ring true, then we must look the same on the inside as we look on the outside. We will be heard with authority to the precise degree that we are willing to put our lives on the line. It is difficult to convince someone of something that we do not believe ourselves. No one is really surprised that revival happened only after Wesley crossed the "ugly ditch" of unbelief at Aldersgate. Those Moravians shortened the leap and made walking beyond sight an exhilarating experience.

There is another aspect to congruency which has sometimes been overlooked. We must not only *believe* what we say, but we must *live* what we preach. Wesley could never have called people throughout the British Isles to scriptural holiness if he had not genuinely sought it himself.

Wesley's character is almost public record. There are two sources which are especially helpful. John Whitehead's *Life of Wesley* includes a section entitled "A Review of Mr. Wesley's Character" and Robert Southey's *Life of Wesley* has an appendix written by Alexander Knox entitled "Remarks on the Life and Character of John Wesley." [9] Both Whitehead and Knox knew Wesley well. Both were close, personal friends. Their accounts are not written in the style of flowery eulogies but are firsthand experiences of a man whose life breathed the same gospel that he preached. Not that Mr. Wesley is portrayed without fault. He is not, but that is what makes these accounts so believable. If we can believe Wesley's weaknesses, we can also believe his strengths. So, I am convinced that there can be little doubt that Wesley was scrupulously moral in an age of rampant immorality. He was refreshingly honest in a time when deceit for many was thought to be the basic ingredient for survival. Knox writes: "On the closest examination, no sentiment, no inclination, will be found to reflect the slightest shade on Mr. Wesley's moral principals or feelings. Whatever mixtures there may be of speculative error or injudicious guidance, the ultimate object is uniformly pure and excellent; be the prescribed means of advancement what they may, the point aimed at is consummate virtue, in every temper and in every action." [10]

For those who knew and loved him best there was never "the slightest breath of suspicion" as to Wesley's "immaculate integrity." [11] Wesley's character was never won at the price of isolation, however. He was forever among the people and they frequently persecuted him for his efforts. Yet "persecution, abuse, or injury he bore from strangers, not only without anger, but without an apparent emotion." [12] Not that he was never sharp or even unkind, especially among his own. Wesley had an active, penetrating mind that could lash out at "his own" in a moment. He had difficulty bearing opposition within the connection. In the face of such opposition without, he wanted close ranks within. Fortunately he was usually quick to see his own unkindness and quick to ask forgiveness. Similarly, he was quick to forgive and thereby released resentment. I have always liked this description in his "Character of a Methodist":

For he is "pure in heart." The love of God has purified his heart from all revengeful passions, from envy, malice, and wrath, from every unkind temper or malign affection. It hath cleansed him from pride and haughtiness of spirit, whereof alone cometh contention, and he hath now "put on bowels of mercies, kindness, humbleness of mind, meekness, long-suffering;" so that he "forbears and forgives if he had a quarrel against any; even as God in Christ hath forgiven him." And indeed, all possible ground for contention, on his part, is utterly cut off. For none can take from him what he desires; seeing he "loves not the world, nor" any of "the things of the world;" being now "crucified to the world, and the world crucified to Him;" being dead to all that is in the world, both to "the lust of the flesh, and the lust of the eye, and the pride of life." For "all his desire is unto God and to the remembrance of His name." [13]

Again there can be little doubt that John Wesley not only described the character of a Methodist, he lived it.

7

Wesley's life spoke of consistency. He was a man of many talents and interests, yet he was surprisingly predictable. Not that he was so different from any of us. He had no special gifts available only to the chosen few. The same Spirit that empowered him is available to us. The same Lord saved him. The same call motivated him. Wesley's greatness was not the result of a curious twist of fate. It was the result of obedience to the same grace available to us all. This can be seen in other areas of his life as well.

Style. Character affects style. Whitehead, who heard him often, described Wesley's preaching style in some detail:

> His attitude in the pulpit was graceful and easy; his action calm and natural, yet pleasing and expressive: his voice not loud but clear and manly; his style neat, simple and perspicuous; and admirably adaptive to the capacity of his hearers. His discourses, in point of composition were extremely different on different occasions. When he gave himself sufficient time for study, he succeeded; but when he did not, he frequently failed. It was indeed manifest to his friends for many years before he died, that his employments were too many, and he preached too often, to appear with the same advantage at all times in the pulpit. His sermons were always short: he was seldom more than half an hour in delivering a discourse, sometimes not so long. His subjects were judiciously chosen; instructive and interesting to the audience, and well adapted to gain attention and warm the heart. [14]

I do not know of an evaluation that speaks more directly than that. Whitehead was never in awe of the man but esteemed the instrument used of God in changing the history of a nation.

When speaking of style, many additional characteristics come immediately to mind. Wesley was open and candid. Read the rules of the Societies and Bands: "Speak freely and plainly"; or "Ask as many and as searching questions as may be, concerning their state, sins, and temptations," to name only two.[15] These and other rules, like the laws of the Medes and Persians, were absolute and irrevocable.

Wesley was punctual. Again, Whitehead comments:

> He had a peculiar pleasure in reading and study; and every literary man knows the force of this passion, how apt it is to make him encroach on the time which ought to be employed in other duties: he had a high relish for polite conversation, especially with pious,

8

learned, and sensible men; but whenever the hour came he was to set out on a journey he instantly quitted any subject or any company in which he might be engaged without any apparent reluctance.[16]

Wesley was also remarkably temperate, unselfishly giving, socially aware, politically sensitive, and undeniably zealous in the care of the whole people called Methodists. His temperament has been described at once as warm, gentle, simple, uniform, tough-minded, fair, and affectionate. Whitehead does well to insist that "his friends and followers have no reason to be ashamed of the name Methodist, he has entailed upon them: as, for an uninterrupted course of years, he has given the world an instance of the possibility of living without wasting a single hour; and of the advantage of a regular distribution of time, in discharging the important duties and purposes of life."[17]

Motivation. Single-minded people expose their motivation quite easily. Wesley was an evangelist. His primary motivation, however, was not to save the lost, although that was certainly important to him. His primary motivation was the love of God and people. Because he loved God and people he was an extraordinary evangelist. Wesley saw the great commission in light of the great commandment.

Wesley, first of all, loved God. His constant fear was that he did not love God enough. He saw full well that the wellspring for genuine ministry found its source in God. So he writes in "The Character of a Methodist":

A Methodist is one who has "the love of God shed abroad in his heart by the Holy Spirit given unto him;" one who "loves the Lord his God with all his heart, and with all his soul, and with all his mind, and with all his strength." God is the joy of his heart, and the desire of his soul; which is constantly crying out, "whom have I in heaven but thee? and there is none upon earth that I desire besides thee! My God and my all! Thou art the strength of my heart, and my portion forever!"[18]

The necessary corollary for all of this was to love one's neighbor as one's self. Again he writes:

He [a Methodist] loves every man as his own soul. His heart is full of love to all mankind, to every child of "the Father of the spirits of all flesh." That a man is not personally known to him, is no bar to his

9

love; no, nor that he is known to be such as he approves not, that he repays hatred for his good-will. For he "loves his enemies;" yea, and the enemies of God, "the evil and the unthankful." And if it be not in his powers to "do good to them that hate him," yet he ceases not to pray for them, though they continue to spurn his love and still "despitefully use him and persecute him." [19]

The point of all this where evangelism is concerned is crucial. Any attempt to win the lost without first loving them smacks of manipulation. Wesley's first approach to people was to love them and then, because he loved them, to lead them to life eternal.

Relevance for today. If the relevance of each model is not applicable for today then we have missed our mark. We have already stated that our goal is not to establish a way of doing things as though nothing has changed. The relevance lies in the precedent of obedience to the same God—yesterday, today, and forever.

The message that Wesley preached is important especially for its emphasis upon grace. Today a great deal is being said about the work of the Holy Spirit. The Holy Spirit still draws, converts, and sanctifies those who place their faith and trust in Jesus Christ as Savior and Lord. Salvation is beyond our grasp but within God's grace. Whatever it takes to communicate the essentials, the essence of that proclamation, is gospel for today as much as in Wesley's day. If that is the message that you feel called to preach, then you stand on giant shoulders.

The relevance for character lies most profoundly in the area of congruency. We must "walk the talk." God has called each of us to "flesh out" the gospel that we preach. Again, if that is your calling, then you stand on giant shoulders.

Style can be mistaken for method. Since method might not yield to a transferable concept, we chose style as an opportunity to speak of certain characteristics such as intensity, candor, and even discipline. While Wesley's particular style will not be our own, the relevance of such traits should be fairly obvious. At any rate, any Methodist evangelist who demonstrates any of these characteristics and holds to their importance, stands on giant shoulders.

Finally, love should certainly be our primary motivation. To begin anywhere else is not only to betray Wesley, but the scriptures as well. Thank God for giant shoulders. In many ways Wesley has taught us well. He is a powerful precedent for much that is profoundly Christian.

Chapter 2: Lay Beginnings

"Extraordinary messengers, raised up to provoke the *ordinary* ones to jealousy."

Minutes of the Conference, 1744

The first evangelists within the connection of Methodists (apart from the Wesleys and George Whitefield) were laymen (and soon afterward, laywomen).[1] The converts to the preaching of Whitefield and the Wesleys were many. The problem was that when they moved on to preach elsewhere, the people fell away so that upon return they were forced to start again, but with less success than before since the second impression was never as strong as the first. Wesley devised a remedy. He would leave a lay person in charge (since no clergy would assist at all). For example, Thomas Maxfield was left responsible for the society in London and was instructed to confirm the newly converted by reading, by praying, or by exhortation.[2]

The development of the lay preacher/evangelist.[3] The transition from exhorting to preaching was a step easily taken. Maxfield's official biographers write that he:

> Being fervent in spirit, and mighty in the Scriptures, greatly profited the people. They crowded to hear him; and, by the increase of their number, as well as by their earnest and deep attention, they insensibly led him to go farther than he had first designed. He began to *preach*; and the Lord so blessed the Word that many were not only deeply awakened and brought to repentance, but were also made happy in a consciousness of pardon. The Scripture marks of true conversion, inward peace, and power to walk in all holiness, evinced the work to be of God.[4]

Upon his return to London, Wesley was at first distressed thinking that Mr. Maxfield had overstepped his bounds. An interesting exchange ensued with his mother, Susanna, who was then living in a house next to the Foundry. Wesley stated rather curtly: "Thomas Maxfield has turned preacher, I find." Susanna, looking at him seriously, replied:

"John, you know what my sentiments have been; you cannot suspect me of favoring readily anything of this kind; but take care what you do with respect to that young man, for he is as surely called of God to preach as you are. Examine what have been the fruits of his preaching and hear him also yourself." [5] As was most often the case, Wesley took his mother's advice. He heard Maxfield preach and was most impressed, realizing instantly that what he himself had begun was bigger than he was. He then stated: "It is the Lord; let Him do what seemeth Him good." [6] Although Wesley seemed obstinate at times, he could change opinions in a flash for the good of the kingdom. He resolved, if he could not break it (this lay preaching), he would harness it in hopes of storming the very gates of hell. He was soon assigning lay preachers to every society. All that he required was that these preachers should submit to his authority to appoint, so that they would not stand in each other's way.

The development of the lay preachers/evangelists looked something like this. Assistants or helpers were appointed by Wesley to govern the societies in his absence. They were to enforce the Rules and direct every part of the discipline as Wesley would have done had he been there himself. These assistants or helpers were then allowed to preach, although Wesley was quick to add that they were never to serve the sacraments. They were lay evangelists, not ministers or priests. [7] Later on, as the work of the Revival expanded, many of these local preachers who would leave their jobs and submit to four years of probation were appointed itinerant or traveling preachers. Here is Wesley's rationale: "My principle (frequently declared) is this, 'I submit to every ordinance of man, wherever I do not conceive there is an absolute necessity for acting contrary to it' consistently with this, I do tolerate lay preaching, because I conceive there is an absolute necessity for it; inasmuch as were it not, thousands of souls would perish everlastingly." [8] Still later Wesley would appoint superintendents and eventually "ordain," but that is a story for our next chapter. For now, what of the qualifications for these early lay preachers?

Qualifications. Traveling evangelists were no novelty in the eighteenth century. Wesley sought to improve their quality by holding them personally (to himself) and mutually (within the connection) accountable. He examined and tested their call, insisting that they submit that call to him and to each other (this caused some of them to separate from the Methodists). He insisted that they obey the Rules of the Society. He encouraged them to improve their minds as well as their gifts. They had to be willing to spend and be spent in the work of the Lord. Let's look closer.

The call of God was crucial. Let me illustrate with the example of an early preacher, John Pawson. His own account is recorded in the *Lives of the Early Methodist Preachers*. I will paraphrase it here with occasional quotations, but you would do well to read the entire account yourself.[9] It is a striking story. Pawson starts out: "Having found salvation myself, I felt an intense desire that others should enjoy the same unspeakable blessing." At that point he began a Sunday evening prayer meeting which was attended by many of his neighbors. As there was no one to bring a word of exhortation, Pawson sometimes read a sermon or the Homilies of the Established Church. The minister of the parish was so offended by the people becoming Methodists that he at first attempted to undermine Pawson's efforts, but being unable to distract him eventually left town. Soon afterward Pawson agreed to read select portions of scripture, attempting to explain them as best he could. His endeavors were so well received that he was made a class leader. This was a turning point.

As a class leader, Pawson experienced more and more of God's grace which gave him an "uninterrupted communion with God." Many were converted including several members of his own family. He was then encouraged to visit the neighboring Societies and give them a word of exhortation. He refused at first, thinking himself unqualified, but the itinerant preacher appointed to that Circuit persuaded him otherwise. Pawson was warned that not to answer God's call was to displease God greatly. Pawson was then placed in the Plan of local preachers. He preached with great success until conference time. The itinerant preacher recommended him as a candidate for traveling preacher. Then these words:

> When Mr. Wesley asked me if I were willing to give up myself to the work, I trembled exceedingly; for I was far from being satisfied that this was the will of the Lord concerning me: however, as I seriously believed that they were a body of men that were under the *divine* infuence, I replied, "I am deeply sensible of my own weakness and insufficiency for so great a work; but if you and the brethren think good to make a trial of me, I give myself to you."[10]

The *Lives of the Early Methodist Preachers* is filled with this and

13

similar stories. Many of those stories develop a familiarity, but all are unique. Wesley insisted: "Every preacher whom God has sent will have a message to some souls who have not been reached by any other." [11] Therefore, he not only examined the call of each of his preachers, he tested it as well. In the Minutes of the Conference, 1770, Wesley inquires:

3 marks

1) Do they know God as a pardoning God? Have they the love of God abiding in them? Do they desire and seek nothing but God? And, are they holy in all manner of conversation? 2) Have they *gifts* (as well as *grace*) for the work? Have they (in some tolerable degree) a clear, sound understanding? Have they a right judgment in the things of God? Have they a just conception of salvation by faith? And, has God given them any degree of utterance? Do they speak justly, readily, clearly? 3) Have they *fruit*? Are any truly convinced of sin and converted to God by their Preaching?

As long as these three marks concur in anyone, we believe he is called of God to preach. These receive as sufficient proof, that he is *moved thereto by the Holy Ghost.*[12]

These same Minutes go on to inquire of probationers:

Have you *faith in Christ*? Are you *going on to perfection*? Do you expect to be *perfected in love in this life*? Are you groaning after it? Are you resolved to devote yourself wholly to God and to His work? Do you know the *Methodist* Plan? Have you read the *Plain Account*, the Appeals? Do you know the *Rules of the Society*? Of the *Bands*? Do you keep them? Do you take no snuff? Tobacco? Drams? Do you constantly attend the church and sacrament? Have you read the Minutes of the Conference? Are you willing to conform to them? Have you considered the *Rules of an Helper*? Especially the first, tenth, and twelfth? Will you keep them for conscience-sake? Are you determined to employ *all* your time in the work of God? Will you preach every morning and evening: endeavoring not to speak too long, or too loud? Will you diligently instruct the children in every place? Will you visit from house to house? Will you recommend fasting, both by precept and example?[13]

Along another line, Wesley not only expected his preachers to demonstrate true spirituality but to improve their minds as well. His well-known remark: "Oh, to reunite the two so long divided: knowledge and vital piety," says it well. He asked his preachers to read and pray at least five hours a day. If they did not want to read and pray five hours a day, they should learn to want to read and pray five hours a day. If they could not learn to want to read and pray five hours a day, then they should return to their trades for they would be triflers the rest of their days and pretty superficial preachers. Not that lay preachers had to be well educated—most were not. Wesley simply expected them to be informed. He wanted growth in every area of life. Little wonder, the badge of cause for the early Methodist preachers was "spend and be spent." Let me explain.

The phrase "spend and be spent" was frequently used by Wesley to describe the life of an evangelist. He writes: "I hope that my life (rather than my tongue) says, I desire only to spend and to be spent in the work." [14] That his preachers picked up on this term is evident by their own willingness to experience incredible hardship. Take, for example, this account from the *Lives of the Early Methodist Preachers* regarding the experience of Thomas Olivers. He tells this story:

One evening, just as I was going into the pulpit at a village about eight miles out of Liverpool, I was seized with a great spitting of blood. However, as I did not know where it might end, I was determined, if possible, to say something for God once more. Accordingly, I began, and delivered a few sentences, and then spit out a great quantity of blood; and so I went on for about half an hour. I then, in the best manner I could, commended myself and the people unto God. And as I did not judge it safe to staab01y that night in a village where help could not be had in case of extreme necessity, I took my horse, and returned to Liverpool. Shortly after I heard that one of the most abandoned and noted sinners in those parts was awakened that night. This made a great noise far or near, and was a means of stopping the mouths of many gainsayers and perhaps of saving some souls from death. On receiving this account, all within me cried out,

"My life, my blood, I here present
if for Thy cause they may be spent:
fulfill Thy sovereign pleasure, Lord!
Thy will be done, Thy name adored." [15]

15

John Pawson's testimony already mentioned includes these words: "I found my mind powerfully drawn to give up myself wholly to God; and from the fullest conviction, that the religion of Jesus Christ is the happiest and best thing in the world, I resolve, in the strength of the Lord, to follow Him, fully, and to spend and be spent in His work." [16] Thus, the qualifications were stiff and the demands great. Such is the calling of an evangelist. Mean little demands yield mean little results. Want to be great? Be a servant of all! Wesley wanted his preachers to be ashamed of nothing but sin. None should be too proud to fetch wood or to draw water or to polish their own shoes or the shoes of their neighbors.[17] Let's conclude this section with Wesley's words: "You think it your duty to call sinners to repentance. Make full proof hereof, and we shall rejoice to receive you as a fellow-labourer." [18]

Pattern and content. On the surface the pattern and content of ministry for the early Methodist evangelists is fairly obvious. They preached a present, personal Savior. They proclaimed the gospel as power unto salvation. They then met with the Societies where all present were exhorted to press on toward perfection. There is, however, a deep truth embedded here which has been overlooked by many. The early Methodist evangelists were never content with barely saving people from hell. They wanted to save from sin as well. *Christian discipleship was their goal.* Let me say more.

Wesley took seriously the words from Ephesians 4:12-13. We are called "to prepare God's people for works of service, so that the body of Christ may be built up until we all reach unity in the faith and in the knowledge of the Son of God and become mature, attaining to the whole measure of the fullness of Christ"(NIV). Wesley became so exasperated with backsliding that he commented late in the Revival: "I would far rather retain than gain." His evangelists were not only to preach, but attach new converts immediately to a lively body. The Societies became nursery for sinners and nurture for saints. In 1747, the question was raised in Conference as to whether or not they should preach in areas where there was no Society. The immediate response was: "Let's try it." The following year the plan was abandoned. Methodists were to preach no more where there was no Society or where no Society could be established. The reason? There was no body to which converts could be attached and, therefore, there was no lasting fruit.

The test then for the effectiveness of an evangelist was not just whether or not sinners were being converted, but whether or not converts were being molded after the image and mind of Christ. Wesley wanted growth by multiplication, not just addition. Every Methodist, lay and clergy alike, was to become a disciple who could then instruct others. "Preparing God's people was the task of the entire Society." Any preachers who did not realize this fully were not worth their salt.

Let's put all of this just a bit differently while at the same time correcting a common misunderstanding. Just because the early Methodist evangelists were, on the whole, lay people and not well educated did not mean that they did not understand the deeper things of the Spirit. Admittedly many lacked sophistication and were not drawn to the clever phrase but, oh, how they could preach the whole gospel! Susanna Wesley once described preaching as meant "to mend men's lives, not to fill their heads with unprofitable speculations." [19] Theology is deep when it makes us deep. In fact, lay preachers were frequently more effective in awakening sinners and confirming saints than those with more cultivated minds. *First*, it was their simplicity. Most of their sermons dealt with repentance toward God, faith toward Christ, and the fruits that follow—righteousness, and peace and joy in the Holy Spirit. Whitehead writes: "To enforce the necessity of repentance, of seeking salvation by grace alone through a Redeemer, the Preacher would often draw a picture of human nature in such strong and natural colours, that everyone who heard him saw his own likeness in it, and was ready to say, he hath shewn me all that was in my heart." [20] *Second*, it was their commitment to holiness. All of Wesley's preachers were exhorted: "Bring as many sinners as you possibly can to repentance, and with all your power to build them up in that holiness, without which they cannot see the Lord." [21] Some interesting statistics have recently surfaced in a Ph.D. dissertation by Tom Albin now being completed toward a degree at Cambridge University. Albin points out that, according to his extensive sampling of early Methodists, nearly 70 percent of those convinced of sin, nearly 60 percent of those converted, and nearly 80 percent of those sanctified were led into those experiences by lay men or lay women. This brings us to our next section.

Early women evangelists. Early in the Revival Wesley encouraged several women called to preach to exhort all within their influence. Unfortunately, the opposition to women preaching became so strong that eventually Wesley withdrew his support publicly, but privately he continued to encourage them in every way.

The first woman preacher among the Methodists was probably Sarah Crosby. Read this advice to her, carefully deciphering between the lines. Wesley writes:

Miss Bosanquet (later Mrs. John Fletcher) gave me yours on Wednes-

17

day night. Hitherto, I think you have not gone too far. You could not well do less. I apprehend all you can do more is, when you meet again, to tell them simply, "you lay me under great difficulty. The Methodists do not allow of women preachers; neither do I take upon me any such character. But I will just nakedly tell you what is in my heart." This will in a great measure obviate the grand objection and prepare for J. Hampson's coming. I do not see that you have broken any law. Go on calmly and steadily. If you have time, you may read to them the *Notes* on any chapter before you speak a few words, or one of the most awakening sermons, as other women have done so long ago.[22]

So Wesley's standard rule became "no women preachers" but in his advice to individuals he exhorted them to "enlarge on certain questions" or to "give a short exhortation," making "short observations."[23] He advises another woman to confer with God, not with flesh and blood, as to how far and in what manner to speak. Satan would keep her silent but she should break through.[24] To still another he states: "You have a message from God to all the women in the Society. Set aside all evil shame, all modesty, falsely so called. Go from house to house; deal faithfully with them all; warn every one; exhort every one. God will everywhere give you a word to speak, and His blessing therewith."[25]

Wesley strongly advises Adam Clarke's wife to exercise the office of deaconess.[26] He tells Hannah Ball and Ann Bolton to itinerate. They must visit the neighboring Societies. "You should not be pinned down to any one place. That is not your calling. Methinks I want you to be (like me) here and there and everywhere. Oh what a deal of work has Our Lord to do on the earth! And may we be workers together with Him!"[27] In spite of Wesley's open policy, we know that there were many such women preachers/evangelists. In his *Journal* he describes a work done in Wells by several women who established a Society there by preaching in the open air (though in peril of life). There were none but women teachers in that Society.[28] The *Proceedings of the Wesley Historical Society* record a permit and authorization to preach for Sally Mallett by an assistant but on order from Wesley himself.[29] Wesley's sermon, "On Visiting the Sick," contains a marvelous word. Read it carefully.

"There is neither male nor female in Christ Jesus." Indeed, it has long past for a maxim with many, that "women are only to be seen,

18

not heard." And accordingly many of them are brought up in such a manner as if they were only designed for agreeable playthings! But is this doing honor to the sex? or is it a real kindness to them? No; it is the deepest unkindness; it is horrid cruelty; it is mere Turkish barbarity. And I know not how any woman of sense and spirit can submit to it. Let all you that have it in your power assert the right which the God of nature has given you. Yield not to that vile bondage any longer! You, as well as men, are rational creatures. You, like them, were made in the image of God; you are equally candidates for immortality; you, too, are called of God, as you have time, to "do good unto all men." Be "not disobedient to the heavenly calling." Whenever you have opportunity, do all the good you can . . .[30]

Relevance for today. With this chapter fresh on my mind, the relevance of all this seems obvious to me. Lest I presume too much, however, let's lift a few points for you to consider in light of our own day.

Just as the evangelists developed out of a grassroots laity, it appears abundantly clear to me that we need to be aware of those being called out of the rank and file. We can exhort and affirm those gifts around us so that the whole body, the church, might be duly strengthened.

Our own qualifications for ministry must be examined and tested in light of their fruit. Are we submitting to our own Methodist discipline? Are we improving our minds as well as our gifts? Have we united the two so long divided: knowledge and vital piety? Are we willing to spend and be spent in the work of the Lord?

Pattern and content speak mainly of simplicity and discipling. Is our presentation of the gospel clear? Are we nurturing those who are being converted? Evangelistic preaching purely for the sake of "winning souls" is a nineteenth century phenomenon. The early Methodist evangelists preached to make disciples. We, too, need to engage more of our constituency. We are called to get people in touch with their own gifts for ministry. Many believe that the "one night stand" is a thing of the past. It might well be that it was not even that. The evangelists who make disciples of Jesus Christ may leave a particular setting, but they leave ministry behind in the lives of those people who bear lasting fruit.

Women in ministry are here to stay. We best acknowledge that fact "lest our prayers be hindered" (Peter 3:7). Giant shoulders are male and female.

I have always liked Wesley's statement: "Give me 100 preachers who fear nothing but sin and desire nothing but God and I care not a straw

19

whether they be clergymen [or clergywomen] or laymen [or laywomen]. Such alone will shake the gates of Hell and set up the Kingdom of Heaven on earth." [31]

During the 1744 Conference when the Methodist preachers asked, "In what light are we to consider ourselves?" it was answered, "As *extraordinary messengers*, raised up to provoke the *ordinary* ones to jealousy." [32] Have we come full circle? Are we the ones now provoked? Let's face it. Maybe the demands asked in this chapter are too great for many of us to bear, but it is at least good to know that there were some who paid the price of greatness. If the truth be known, some of us might well have to do it again.

Chapter 3: Ordination

Sep. 1, 1784. '4 Prayed, Ordained R[ichard] Whatcoat and T[homas] Vasey
Sep. 2. '4 Prayed, Ordained Dr. Coke!'"

John Wesley's Diary

Although I am certain that John Wesley never intended it, the ordination of his lay preachers/evangelists at some point became inevitable. The image of the man rowing a boat is immensely appropriate. While facing in one direction his every stroke takes him in the other. In fact the situation in America caused Wesley to initiate the ordination himself. Following the Revolutionary War, anything ecclesiastical, political, or otherwise, that still smacked of the Crown, carried with it the "kiss of death." Independence applied to the church as well as to the state. Although the established church took on the name Episcopal, their methods for survival in a new country were for the most part unimaginative, naive, and a bit paternalistic. No, a new country needed a fresh start. With few ordained ministers willing or able to meet the demands of the rapidly growing Methodist Societies, Wesley (forever the pragmatist) met the demand. He ordained several of his lay preachers/evangelists, first for America and then for Scotland and England as well. Before any such move could be made, however, an interesting pilgrimage had to be made in the mind of Wesley. He had to move from High Church Anglican to renegade Bishop of a movement at once destined for continuity and discontinuity with the work begun at Oxford over fifty years earlier. The story is both complex and intriguing and, in light of its significance for the evangelists, deserves a closer look.

Wesley at first strongly resisted the ordination of any of his lay preachers, as this would free them to act as pastors/ministers (administering the sacraments, etc.) and thereby cutting the knot with the Established Church. In chapter two we quoted Wesley saying that he tolerated lay preaching because of its absolute necessity lest thousands should perish. The words to follow that statement shed light on the present question: "Yet I do not tolerate lay administering, because I do not conceive there is any such necessity for it; seeing it does not appear, that one soul will perish for want of it."[1]

In his sermon "The Ministerial Office" Wesley insists that in the New Testament evangelists and pastors are separate offices. He writes: "I cannot prove from any part of the New Testament, or from any author of the three first centuries, that the office of an Evangelist gave any man a right to act as a Pastor or Bishop."[2] The context for this sermon is interesting. It was preached in Ireland where several preachers had assumed that since they had been appointed to "preach the gospel" they had the right also to administer the sacraments without any further appointment. Wesley reminds them that they had been set apart only to preach. They should confine themselves to that part of the work to which they had been appointed. Ordination was not the issue. In fact, thirty preachers had by this time (1789) already been ordained by Wesley himself that they might administer the sacraments. The point here is that lay preachers should not serve the sacraments without credentials to do so. So, how did our lay preachers/evangelists become ordained? The story lengthens.

Sons in the Gospel. Wesley was fond of referring to his preachers as "Sons in the Gospel." These had been "set apart" to preach. This setting apart was an ordination of sorts. It was an ordination (or setting apart) to preach with the words: "Take thou authority to preach the gospel." They were, however, to go no further. Nonetheless this first "ordination" or "setting apart" was crucial for that which would follow. For now, however, this (thought Wesley) was sufficient for the cause of revival.

Wesley did not want to separate from the Church of England. He had studied previous renewal movements (Presbyterians, Independents, Anabaptists, Quakers) and had concluded that they were mistaken to separate. They scarcely did any good, except to their own little body. They aroused prejudice against themselves and thereby totally cut off the hope of a general, national reformation.[3]

Admittedly Wesley's reasons not to separate were prudential only. Wesley wanted to renew, restore, revitalize, reform the whole. Leaven was no good outside the lump. He had no desire to create or originate a new order, only to purify or perfect the old after the pattern of the Primitive Church.[4]

So, Wesley rightly saw the significance of the sacraments. They were the umbilical cord back to the mother church. As long as Methodists were dependent upon the Established Church for the sacraments, the link was fairly secure.

Yet, in spite of all this, the evangelists continued to develop in their importance. Wesley's "Sons in the Gospel" soon became assistants.[5] These "Sons" were vital to the revival efforts. As they proved themselves leaders among the few, they were entrusted with greater responsibility. As seen in chapter two, these assistants began to itinerate. The itineracy insured the *connection*. The Societies needed to be linked together. In fact there were few pioneer evangelists after the first decade of the Revival except at the request of some local Society. These lay evangelists were expected primarily to secure, nurture, and consolidate.

In 1744 the connection became known as the *conference* (more will be said later as to the importance of the conference). This first conference was attended by six clergy. Four lay preachers were also asked by Wesley to join them. At the time, there were forty lay preachers in all. The next year there were fifty lay preachers and fifteen of these were appointed assistants. These assistants (full-time traveling preachers) would eventually become the candidates for ordination.[6] By 1747 the number of assistants had grown to twenty-three (there were thirty-eight local preachers). After 1749 these assistants were appointed to circuits. It was during this same period that Wesley became more and more open to some rather startling new insights that would affect both the status and the role of the evangelist.

Ecclesiastical experimentation. Interestingly enough, the ordination of Wesley's lay evangelists resulted from his persistent views that lay preachers should never serve the sacraments. The sacraments could be administered only by the appointed elders or priests. Had lay evangelists never been ordained, the Methodists would have ceased to be a movement of real significance following Wesley's death. The American Methodists, for example, would have been cut off, with little access to the ordained ministry. Although Wesley never changed his views that ordained clergy alone should serve the sacraments, he became convinced during this period (the 1740s) that *he* could ordain if the necessity presented itself.

Wesley's early bias was High-Church Anglican. There were three distinct orders — deacon, elder (presbyter), and bishop. Each required a separate ordination and consecration as a higher order. Then in 1746, a sudden change of mind is recorded in his journal. After reading Lord King's account of the *Primitive Church* he writes: "In spite of the vehement prejudice of my education, I was ready to believe that this was a fair and impartial draught; but, if so, it would follow that bishops and presbyters are (essentially) of one order, and that originally every

23

Christian congregation was a church independent of all others!" [7] What's this? If elders and bishops are essentially the same order, then Wesley as elder could also ordain as bishop. Bishop Stillingfleet's *Irenicum* reinforced this same view, although Stillingfleet was suggesting that this would be appropriate only in a case of emergency. [8]

At first Wesley did not choose to use the authority within him because he was convinced (as suggested earlier) that no group that withdrew from the established church had left a lasting mark upon the masses. To ordain his Methodists would sever the one remaining tie with the Established Church.

The next thirty-five years evidenced many changes, however, that forced Wesley to reconsider his willingness to use such authority. An emergency situation had presented itself. When Wesley had explored every orthodox channel for solving the problem, he felt free to look elsewhere. Pragmatic spirituality mattered far more than outward patterns of ecclesiastical organization. He began to experiment with several alternatives. Although he continued to look over his shoulder to see if anyone was accusing him of abandoning the "old plan" (to stay within the Established Church) for a "new plan" (to separate), Wesley did two things. First, he drew up a Deed of Declaration. This increased the importance of the Conference and tightened the connection into an effective tool for spreading scriptural holiness throughout the land. Second, he chose in extreme cases to ordain.

1784, the Deed of Declaration. Late in the Revival the Methodists had built preaching houses for their Societies throughout the British Isles. This meant that, increasingly, there was a need to protect their property from splinter groups who might want to pull out and establish their own fellowships apart from the Societies that had established them. Also Wesley was now eighty-one years of age and there needed to be some provision for his succession. As usual when a need arose, Wesley was quick to meet that need. Thus he drew up the Deed of Declaration. This was its effect.

I mentioned earlier that the Methodist connection of Societies had become a Conference in 1744. This strengthened the role of the Methodist preacher/evangelist. Although Wesley himself still made final decisions, more and more responsibility was given to these preachers within their appointed circuits. Now, forty years later, the Deed of Declaration made this connection of preachers (there were 100 members with 40 needed for a *quorum*) a separate body. Although the Methodists still viewed themselves as a part of the Established Church, they were now a legally identifiable organization. Wesley intended that following his death the power which had long been his alone would be transferred to the Conference. Wesley now became president of that Conference. From this point on, the Conference itself would establish final authority in Methodist polity.[9]

Membership in this Conference would become the key to ordination. The full-time assistants were those who exhibited (1) true Christian faith and character, (2) gifts (as well as grace), and (3) an effectiveness in preaching as evangelists. These were accepted into *full-connection*. Eventually, after Wesley's death, ordination simply meant entering into full-connection, but first there is an interim story.

Of necessity. By the time of the Deed of Declaration there was an almost desperate need for ordained preachers in America. There were 15,000 Methodists in Societies but there were no ordained Methodist preachers to serve them. After the war there were few Anglican priests and no bishops (America being a part of the diocese of London). Some preachers (like Robert Strawbridge) began to administer the sacraments but did so "illegally" and the Societies were threatening to split. Wesley at first appealed to Dr. Lowth, the bishop of London, to ordain a Methodist for America, but the Bishop refused.[10]

Wesley now believed it was time for him to exercise an authority which he had believed for many years to be within his power—to ordain. Raymond George, in his chapter entitled "Ordination" in *A History of the Methodist Church in Great Britain*, writes that Wesley decided to ordain on at least two principles.[11] First, Wesley states: "I am now as firmly attached to the Church of England as I ever was since you knew me. But meantime I know myself to be as real a Christian bishop as the Archbishop of Canterbury." [12] Second, he appeals to Lord King, Bishop Stillingfleet, and the Church of Alexandria where presbyters consecrated new bishops for vacant sees.[13] George states that Stillingfleet in particular thought that the power to ordain was intrinsically in presbyters (elders) but that this should be exercised only in case of necessity. Wesley thought that this was such a case. So, on September 1, 1784, with Thomas Coke and James Creighton (priests in the Church of England) to assist him, John Wesley, in order to fill the ecclesiastical vacuum in America, ordained the first Methodist evangelists. They were Richard Whatcoat and Thomas Vasey who were ordained deacon and elder on successive days. Thomas Coke was then ordained as "superintendent." The term *superintendent* was clearly intended to carry the weight of *bishop* since the words used in his consecration were similar to the ones used for the consecration of the bishop in the Book of Common Prayer, 1662. Coke was then expected to ordain in turn once in America. Accordingly Coke ordained Francis Asbury deacon, elder, and superintendent on successive days after his arrival in America, but that is the story of Part II. For now, we will remain in Great Britain.

It is interesting to note that on the certificate of ordination Wesley used the words *set apart* but in his private diary the word *ordained* is used. Remember that earlier Wesley had "set apart" his assistants only to preach. Now he was setting them apart to serve in full capacity as pastors or ministers of the gospel.[14] The sequence is logical. Just as it had been necessary to employ lay preachers to strengthen his own hands in meeting the demands of the Revival, it was now necessary to ordain some of these same lay preachers/evangelists in order to carry on the next phase of Methodism—a separate church in America.

A new thing. In all Wesley ordained at least twenty-seven men.[15] Thirteen were ordained for overseas, eleven for Scotland, and three "special cases" for England. These "special cases" now draw our attention.

Wesley's justification for the ordination of those to serve abroad is relatively straightforward. There was a need that only ordained Methodist preachers/evangelists could meet. Even the situation in Scotland is fairly clear. There the established church was Presbyterian, not Anglican. Furthermore, many of the Presbyterian ministers refused to administer the sacraments to the Methodists until they recanted their Methodist beliefs. In light of the Arminian flavor of Methodism and the Reformed character of Presbyterianism, this cut to the heart of what most Methodists deemed vital to faith and action. In 1785, therefore, three men were ordained for Scotland, although these ordainees were to act as such only in Scotland. Then exactly three years later Wesley ordained Alexander Mather for England.

The English scene was different. Here the Methodists had full access to the sacraments. So, how did Wesley justify this ordination?

In 1788 Wesley ordained Alexander Mather who clearly was to remain in England. This was a "new principle."[16] For many, Wesley's rationale seems hazy. Let's look closer.

John Simon sheds a great deal of light on this subject.[17] Wesley was now feeling the effects of his years. To an extent the die had already been cast. Wesley must have known that he had brought his followers too far to turn back now. Although he would not allow separation in his own lifetime, he made certain that the people called Methodists could

26

perpetuate themselves if and when the separation occurred. The machinery was already in motion. The move from connection to Conference was first. Now the move from the ordination of preacher to the ordination of priest was the next logical step if Methodism was to be sustained.

Some would also argue that the focus was now moving across the Atlantic. It is abundantly clear, for example, that Thomas Coke was attempting to bring British Methodism in line with the American church.[18] My friend Tom Albin argues that ordination for Wesley was the death rather than the culmination of his ultimate dream. Wesley simply came to terms with reality. His desire was to renew the Established Church within, but he was nonetheless unwilling to allow souls to perish for the sake of ecclesiastical propriety.

After Wesley. John Wesley died in 1791. In the year following his death no official ordination was performed, although a few preachers were ordained informally and served the sacraments against the ruling of the Conference. The Conference itself had been geared to succeed Wesley. In 1793 the Conference decided that the distinction between ordained and unordained preachers should be dropped. Although Thomas Coke attempted to make a case for a British episcopacy within Methodism, this was rejected as tending to create "invidious and unhallowed distinctions among brethren."[19] The controversy in these years still surrounded the administration of the sacraments. The issue was still unclear. Then in 1795 the *Plan of Pacification* settled it once and for all. The Conference ruled through this plan that all traveling preachers in full-connection could serve the sacraments. In effect, *full-connection implied ordination.* Although the laying on of hands was not introduced as a part of ordaining rubric until 1836 (except by Coke for those going overseas), Methodism was now (although Methodism never formally separated) a church unto itself.[20]

John Simon quotes John Pawson, now bishop of Scotland, to the effect that if the Methodist preachers could have served the sacraments quietly, no division would have occurred. The question then is: How does one shout quietly? Surely Pawson must have realized the import of all of this. Again, the knot was cut. The Societies were now churches served by their own preachers and accountable to their own church government alone.

One closing comment is important. The evangelist, lay or ordained, was always closely associated with the Societies. Although they traveled, they were attached to a circuit. They were servants of the body

27

and accountable to it. To my knowledge there were few if any evangelists at large. This came about later, after Methodism began to lose its evangelistic fervor so that "independent" evangelists were called in on occasion to raise that particular standard. By 1800, for example, much of Methodism had already become self-conscious about its early enthusiasm. Even men as notable as Thomas Rankin (ordained by Wesley himself in 1789) can be found "cleaning up" an earlier autobiography by omitting certain emotional trappings. Interestingly enough, Asbury would later refer to Rankin as Diotrephes (one seeking pre-eminence in the church).

Relevance for today. It is not intended here to imply that all of the Methodist preachers/evangelists were ordained. Those willing to travel and willing to submit to the appointment of the Conference were ordained by virtue of their admission into full-connection. Many evangelists, however, chose to carry on locally as they continued in their trades. Business occupied them by day; the gospel occupied them by night. Today, we have been too dependent at times upon the ordained. Many of us who are ordained do not object to lay evangelists. We welcome more harvesters for the harvest. Many lay people can preach effectively without either appointment or ordination. We need to encourage them. Our ordained system is too closely tied to our educational system. We sometimes fail to affirm gifts that do not demonstrate the sophistication of seminary training. Surely there is not only room enough but need for all of us.

Wesley ordained not to make better evangelists, but to perpetuate a movement. We forget that most of our heritage is linked with the laity. Our credentials should not rest in our academic pursuits but in our gifts (and grace). Wesley himself held power not just in his ordination as presbyter, but as leader of the people called Methodists. He was not a bishop by appointment but he was a bishop by virtue of his gifts (and grace). He manifested the fruit of a scriptural bishop. When people made demands upon him as an ordained minister that were too much for him alone, he ordained others to assist him and their fruit was good. The fruit—that is the mark of an evangelist, not ordination. Wesley would not care a fig if it looked like a grapevine; if it produced apples, he called it an apple tree. An evangelist is marked by his or her ability to win the lost for Jesus Christ and it matters not whether they be bishop, elder, deacon, or laity. Such is our calling and such is our need to serve.

28

Part II
The American Scene

Chapter 4:
The Francis Asbury Model

January 1, 1772. I find that the preachers have their friends in the
cities, and care not to leave them. There is a strange party-spirit.
For my part I desire to be faithful to God and man. On Thursday
evening, I preached . . . on I Thess. v. 6: "Let us not sleep as do
others, but let us watch and be sober."

Francis Asbury's *Journal*

The contrasts and similarities between Wesley and Asbury are startling. Few others could be compared so favorably with Wesley in the
advancement of Methodism. In 1771, at the age of twenty-six, Asbury
left England for America. Upon arrival he simply took charge,
strengthening the Societies, establishing a church, preaching the old
Methodist doctrines, spending and being spent for the next forty-five
years. Asbury was the only English Methodist preacher to remain in
America during the War for Independence. When the war ended in
1783, Wesley was forced to take a fresh accounting of American Methodism. During the war years (1776-1783) the Societies had actually
tripled. The resiliency of Methodism was astounding. The number of
preachers had grown from 24 to 82, the circuits from 12 to 39, and the
membership from 4,921 to 13,740.[1] Asbury gathered, exhorted, organized, discipled, and disciplined the people called Methodist. He literally walked out the land for the cause of scriptural holiness. He visited
nearly every state in the Union every year. Like Wesley, he was jealous
over his flock. Like Wesley, he established a style of ministry suited to
the people, to their love for democracy, and to the country in which
they lived. Yet, unlike Wesley, Asbury was virtually self-taught. He left
school before he was twelve to be an apprentice in a forge. Unlike
Wesley, he published little. Nonetheless, although he lacked the polish,
he lacked not the wit; he lacked the sophistication but not the quick-
ness of mind; he lacked the theological training but not the depth of
spirit of Wesley himself. Like Wesley (no doubt following the good man's
precedent), he was doggedly determined to live wholly for God.

We discussed earlier the principle for a model. Again, this is not to
say how it must be done. Asbury, like Wesley, provides a precedent as

31

an evangelist. As with Wesley, let's look at his message, character, style, motivation, and relevance for today.

Message. Asbury's testimony is recorded in his *Journal.*[2] There he tells us that he was "awakened" (made aware of sin and of his need for faith in Christ) before the age of fourteen. He was then quickly drawn to the Methodists. He writes:

> I began to inquire of my mother who, where, what were the Methodists? She gave me a favourable account and directed me to a person that could take me to Wednesbury to hear them. I soon found this was not the Church—but it was better. The people were so devout—men and women kneeling down—saying *Amen.* Now, behold! Why, strange to tell! The preacher had no prayer-book, and yet he prayed wonderfully! What was yet more extraordinary, the man took his text and had no sermon-book: thought I, this is wonderful indeed! It is certainly a strange way, but the best way.[3]

Asbury was converted shortly afterward and joined a class and band within the Methodist Society. In time he started preaching (sometimes three to five times a week) while pursuing his trade. Then between the ages of twenty-one and twenty-two he became a local preacher and eventually entered into full-connection.

Asbury was an exceptional evangelist. Not that he was always successful—he was not. Nearly half the time he reports that his response was dull. Yet, preaching the gospel was his life's blood. He arose to preach in the morning (frequently at 5:00) and preached before going to bed at night. Having no predetermined corpus of sermons, he preached to a particular need and rarely less than an hour.

Although there are 175 sermon outlines recorded in his *Journal,* it is difficult to know for certain exactly what Asbury preached. He rarely wrote out his sermons (although he was not ill-prepared). He published no sermons, tracts, or treatises.[4] Yet we know the nature of his preaching. His message was solemn, penetrating, and *biblical.* He would pray: "Lord, keep me from preaching empty stuff to please the ear, instead of changing the heart!"[5] The Word of God for Asbury was a matter of life and death to his hearers.

Although we do not know exactly what he preached, we do know that the scriptures provided the base for all of his preaching. Asbury cites 700 texts in his *Journal.* In the index of sermon texts he lists 30 of the Old Testament books and 26 of the New Testament books (only

Philemon is omitted). There are 99 references to the Psalms and 135 references to Isaiah alone. The texts are usually brief (two to three verses). Although his method was not so much exegetical, he would take the wording of the text and reconstruct a topical outline suited for a particular audience. Frequently referring to the historical background of a text, on most occasions he would select a passage that could be applied specifically, if not literally, and then seek to enforce it plainly and simply.

Take, for example, the outline for Galatians 6:14: "But far be it from me to glory except in the cross of our Lord Jesus Christ, by which the world has been crucified to me, and I to the world." Asbury writes:

Having obtained more knowledge of the people, my subject was Gal. vi, 14, plain and pointed: my audience was serious and atten-tive. I endeavoured to show,
    1.   what is it for a man to glory in a thing.
    2.   what men glory in, which is not the cross of Christ.
    3.   what is it to glory in the cross of Christ.
    4.   how a person may know when he glories in the cross of Christ—namely, by the world's being crucified to Him, and He unto the world.[6]

Still another outline reveals even more of Asbury's Bible-oriented message. The battle, for Asbury, was not just against flesh and blood. Americans knew a great deal about war, but Asbury wanted victory over sin as well. The Book of Revelation grew in importance to him. He writes for January 14, 1793:

I preached in the new house at Grant's, on "He that overcometh shall inherit all things, and I will be His God, and he shall be My son" [Revelation 21:7].
    1.   The Christian soldier has to overcome the world, sin, and the devil, with his temptations.
    2.   He fights under the banner of Christ, who is the Captain of his salvation.
    3.   His armour is described by St. Paul, Ephes. vi. [Asbury was fond of biblical illustrations].
    4.   His inheritance—Christian tempers, and the things prom-ised to the seven Churches; and finally glory—"will be his God"—giving him wisdom, truth, love—"He shall be my son"—a son

partakes of the nature and property of the father, and doeth his will; so it is with those who are the children of God.[7]

Like Wesley, Asbury was steeped in the Word. He memorized most of the New Testament. Yet, he wanted the Word applied. It had to be relevant. He was constantly looking for situations that would tie the scriptures in with life itself. If people were forced to guard their homes, why not their souls.[8] If they could turn out at 2:00 in the morning to fight a fire, what of the general judgment?[9]

We stated earlier that Asbury was not ill-prepared when delivering his message. As a matter of course, we find him throughout his *Journal* spending time in prayer and meditation. A typical example is November 22, 1779: "Rose between four and five, spent an hour in prayer and meditation. Read a few chapters in the Bible before it was day-light: I want to be all devoted to God; every moment given up to Christ."[10] Immediately he rode to Mr. Maxfield's (a Methodist in Delaware) where he preached to about 300 on Luke 13:23: "Lord, are there few that be saved?" He writes on that occasion:

First, showed, What we are to be saved from.
2. How we are saved.
3. Why there are few. No open sinner can be in a state of salvation; no formalist, violate sectarian, having only opinions and modes of religion; no hyprocrites or backsliders; nor those who are only seekers.[11]

Asbury believed that the best way to prepare for preaching was to commune with God. He was always seeking to improve his time by prayer, meditation, and reading the scriptures.[12] Not that he read nothing else—he did, and constantly. The primary impetus for preaching, however, was *grace*. Whatever opened that door was time well invested. Again, he writes:

I have great discoveries of my defects and weaknesses. My soul is not so steadily and warmly devoted to the Lord as it might be. Lord, help me, and supply me with grace always! In preaching from Ephesians ii, 12, 13, I had great freedom. It seems strange, that sometimes, after much premeditation and devotion, I cannot express my thoughts with readiness and perspicuity; whereas at other times, proper sentences of Scripture and apt expressions occur without care or much thought. Surely this of the Lord. To convince us that it is not by power or might, but by his Spirit the work must be done. Nevertheless, it is doubtless our duty to give ourselves to prayer and meditation, at the same time depending entirely on the grace of God, as if we had made no preparation.[13]

This depending upon grace was never an excuse for indulgence or laziness, however. It was crucial that the message which he proclaimed came first from God. Once when preaching at Yale University he endeavored to show: "(1) what we must be saved from; (2) what has been esteemed by the men of the world as the wisdom of preaching; (3) what is meant by the foolishness of preaching. When I had done, no man spoke to me."[14] Such was the frequent response of the educated which was indicative of their turn of mind, even among those who knew that faith does not rest in the wisdom of men, "but in the power of God" (1 Cor. 2:5).

If Asbury's preaching was biblical, prepared in the fire of whole-hearted devotion to God, it was also theological. His messages covered the full range of Methodist doctrines. Early on, Asbury was convinced that the Methodist understanding of how one relates to God was best. He writes in 1771 on board ship bound for America: "The people God owns in England are the Methodists. The doctrines they preach, and the discipline they enforce, are, I believe, the purest of any people now in the world. The Lord has greatly blessed these doctrines and this discipline in the three kingdoms: they must therefore be pleasing to Him. If God does not acknowledge me in America, I will soon return to England. I know my views are upright now: may they never be otherwise."[15]

To study Asbury's sermon texts and outlines is to realize quickly that several topics receive repeated emphasis. He sought to convict or awaken. He preached repentance and justification. He exhorted perseverance and good works. He warned against backsliding. He emphasized sanctification and going on to perfection. These recurring themes dominated his preaching.

Like Wesley, Asbury chose his texts to suit the situation of the people in front of him. For those unawakened, he selected a text calculated to sober if not to raise the hair. He could not bear carelessness among his listeners. Texts such as Ezek. 33:4 and Zeph. 1:12 were frequently used to arouse those who slept.

For those awakened he preached repentance and justification. Texts such as 1 Tim. 1:15: "This saying is sure and worthy of full acceptance, that Christ Jesus came into the world to save sinners"; Luke 11:13:

"Woe to you, Chorazin! woe to you, Bethsaida! for if the mighty works done in you had been done in Tyre and Sidon, they would have repented long ago, sitting in sackcloth and ashes"; and Luke 19:10: "For the Son of Man came to seek and to save the lost," were used over and over again.

For those converted, he preached perseverance and good works; he warned against backsliding, but mostly within the context of sanctification. As he grew older, Asbury vowed that every sermon he preached would in some way touch on sanctification. He stated: "I find no preaching does good, but that which properly presses the use of the means, and urges holiness of heart; these points I am determined to keep close to in all my sermons." [16]

Sanctification meant, in the simplest terms, dying to sin and coming alive to righteousness as the marks of Christian maturity. Asbury wanted first love changed into perfect love. He feared backsliding as much as Wesley.[17] He feared antinomianism just as much. John Fletcher's *Checks to Antinomianism* were constantly with him. Holiness did not deny the law. It fulfilled the law, not by works, but by grace. He writes in his *Journal* for February 10, 1785: "Rode to Salisbury, where, as it was court time, I had but few hearers; and some of these made their escape when I began to insist on the necessity of holiness—a subject which the Antinomians do not like to hear pressed too closely." [18] The following testimony is typical. On May 18, 1780, Asbury writes:

I was much tired on the way, my horse lame and the road rough; but I lifted up my heart to God. The family sent out and called in about 60 people, black and white. Spoke on Rev. xxii, 13-18. I had liberty, and felt a moving in my own soul. Two women were cut to the heart and were in an agony of soul for holiness: I prayed with them twice, while the people stayed, and afterwards spoke to them: they both, notwithstanding their agony, had a clear sense of the blessing they stood in need of, and believed God had purified their hearts; I saw them both happily breathing a Divine calm and heavenly sweetness. I see clearly that to press the people to holiness, is the proper method to take them from contending for ordinances, or any less consequential things.[19]

To conclude this section on the message we must mention Asbury's balance regarding the lively social issues of his day, especially slavery. The Methodist rules against slavery were not always received peacefully. In fact, Asbury was attacked on several occasions due to his outspokenness. Bishop Coke finally softened his remarks against slavery, but Asbury kept up the attack until he too, for fear of losing many Methodists altogether, began to seek alternative ways to apply pressure against this tyranny of mankind.[20]

Character. True greatness for God does not always avoid the whisper of scandal. Asbury was attacked for many things, but his character was never in question. Although he never married, he was apparently celibate in mind as well as body. His passion was for the souls of people in general and the Methodists in particular. He was unquestionably honest in word and deed. Those who attacked him usually did so in regard to his use of power. On most occasions he answered them well. When one of his critics compared him to the Pope, he responded:

> I will make a few observations upon the ignorance of foolish men, who will rail against our Church government. The Methodists acknowledge no superiority but what is founded on seniority, election, and long and faithful services. For myself, I pity those who cannot distinguish between a pope of Rome, and an old, worn man of about 60 years, who has the *power given him* of riding 5,000 miles a year, at a salary of 80 dollars, through summer's heat and winter's cold, traveling in all weather, preaching in all places; his best covering from rain often but a blanket; the surest sharpener of his wit, hunger—from fast, voluntary and involuntary; his best fare, for 6 months of the 12, coarse kindness; and his reward, suspicion, envy, and murmurings all the year round.[21]

Asbury, like most of us, was not without temptation. If we read carefully, most of his trials seemed to be related to the interruption of his study and devotion. Let me give a few examples. In the spring of 1778 he writes: "I have lately been grievously haunted by the temptations of Satan; but my desire is to die rather than live to sin against God. Lord, stand by me in the day of trial, and every moment support my feeble soul! On Saturday also my mind was much harrassed by my spiritual adversity; and my study and devotion were interrupted, so that I could do but little either for God or myself." [22] During this same period he writes: "My spiritual exercises have been various. I have frequently been under powerful temptations: but at other times my soul has been serene and comfortable. Much of my time is spent in study. And my desire is, to glorify God in all I do, and spend all I gain in His service." [23] Again, he writes: "My practice is, to keep close to God in prayer and spend a part of every hour when awake, in that exercise. . . . My exercises are very deep and various. The Lord makes great discoveries of my defects and shortcomings in many points. He melts my heart into humility and tenderness; He graciously draws me nearer and nearer to himself; and fills me with the spirit of holy love." [24] Let me make just two observations. First, Asbury seems to have been able to conquer temptation by keeping close to God. This "sweet communion" had its highs and lows, but nonetheless seemed to sustain him. He gives this rather remarkable testimony:

My soul was, for the most part, in peace; though at times my own trials and the trials of others produced strong agonies of mind. But strengthened with Divine might, I am able to oppose the tempter in his most violent assaults, and am brought off more than conqueror. The study of the Holy Scriptures affords me great pleasure. Lord, help me to dig into the Gospel field as for hidden treasure! [25]

Second, it is interesting to note that temptation for Asbury can usually be associated with certain periods in his life, most often during times of inactivity. The quotations above were taken from the pen of Asbury while he was in virtual exile in Delaware. These were the war years when it was sometimes difficult for an Englishman to preach. Listen to his words when he dared to leave his sanctuary: "Ventured to leave my asylum; and under the special providence of God, came safe to my old abode; where I purpose spending these perilous days in retirement, devotion, and study. I want for nothing but more holiness, and wonder at the love and care of Almighty God, towards such a dead dog as I am. My spirit was greatly comforted by Psalm cvi, 10: 'He saved them from the hand of him that hated them: and redeemed them from the hand of the enemy.'" [26] It appears that Asbury was most attuned to God during periods of greatest activity. Added discipline was one method of warding off temptation when he was least active. He resolved: "I purposed to rise at four o'clock as often as I can, and spend 2 hours in prayer and meditation; two hours in reading, and one in recreating and conversation; and in the evening, to take my room at eight, pray and meditate an hour, and go to bed at nine o'clock: all this I purpose to do, when not traveling; but to rise at four o'clock every morning." [27]

All of this is not to say that Asbury did not have his faults. By his own admission he struggled continually. To read between the lines in his *Journal* is to suspect that he was tempted with pride and fought it at every turn. Some of the quotations above suggest as much. We also know that Wesley questioned his use of the title "Bishop." This grieved Asbury greatly, yet when all was said and done, he felt justified and sought simply to humble himself before Almighty God.

Style. "Holy boldness" perhaps best characterizes the style of Francis Asbury. He was truly ready to apply God's Word at every opportunity. I like this account: "A poor, unhappy man abused me much on the road: he cursed, swore, and threw stones at me. But I found it my duty to talk to him, and show him his danger." [28] Wesley said, "Go into every house." Asbury added: "Go into every kitchen and shop; address all, aged and young, on the salvation of their souls." [29]

Asbury was first an evangelist. Nathan Bangs makes this comment on his preaching:

It is said by those who had the privilege of hearing him in the vigor of mankind before time and care had wrinkled his forehead, that he was deep and systematical in his discourses, ably and "rightly dividing the Word of Truth," fluent and powerful in his delivery, as well as remarkably pointed in his appeals to the consciences of his hearers. His attitude in the pulpit was graceful, dignified, and solemn; his voice full and commanding; his enunciation clear and distinct; and sometimes a sudden burst of eloquence would break forth in a manner which spoke a soul full of God and like a mountain torrent swept all before it. [30]

Those who knew Asbury best stated that there was a rich variety in his sermons. There was no tedious sameness, no repeating of old stale truths, no cant words to dampen his freshness. Asbury criticized those who were shackled by their notes. He sought carefully not to make the same mistake himself. [31] He also insisted on some sort of invitation at the close of every service whereby the people who were responding might be exhorted more privately.

Asbury's style was to go where the people were. Since America was mostly agrarian, he probed, preached, and prayed among the people outside the cities.

Asbury longed for true revival. His pulse quickened when he sensed that the Holy Spirit was about to break through in a new way. He was particularly sensitive to what was happening in the South where nearly 90 percent of the Methodists lived after the War. He records this in his *Journal:* "God is at work in this part of the country; and my soul catches the holy fire already." [32]

The camp meetings were also a source of inspiration to Asbury. He grew impatient with the Presbyterians who wanted God to work alone.[33] He wanted results, not in the hundreds, not in the thousands, but in the millions.[34] The Methodists, he insisted, were not to be intimidated by noise and intensity. Eventually Asbury sought to bring the enthusiasm of the camp meeting back across the Appalachians and domesticate it for the work of the church in cooler places. He exhorted one of his presiding elders: "I wish you would also hold camp meetings; they have never been tried without success. To collect such a number of God's people together to pray, and the ministers to preach, and the longer they stay, generally, the better—this is field fighting, this is fishing with a large net."[35] Asbury wanted order, but with room enough for liveliness. How else to shake the careless out of their "sleep unto death"?

Before concluding this section it should also be noted that Asbury was an evangelist (and perhaps a prophet), but he was also to become a bishop. Prior to 1784 he was a catalyst for much of what was happening in early American Methodism. Ordination simply acknowledged that fact among men and empowered him to secure the movement.

Whether or not Asbury abused his power, perhaps only God knows. We know, however, that he insisted that he be voted into the position of bishop by the conference (a wise move in light of the new appreciation for American democracy). We also know that he expected no special courtesy. He slept on floors and was frequently highly self-critical. On one occasion he stated that he was "ashamed of himself."[36] Interesting words for a bishop. Nonetheless, as bishop he did demand discipline. Nominal membership was not to be tolerated. This made him enemies, but John Wesley had set a pretty good precedent for such abuse and for many of the same reasons.

Motivation. As an evangelist Asbury believed and taught that prevenient grace made conversion man's business. As a result of free will men and women had to respond. Here was motivation enough for the evangelist. Even as bishop he wrote: "Little sleep last night. Let me suffer and let me labour; time is short, and souls are daily lost."[37] Time was short. The task was great. God, however, was faithful to those who obeyed. Once again Asbury wrote: "The Lord hath enabled me, of late, to be faithful to the families which have come in my way. And we must overcome our natural bashfulness and backwardness, to assist the precious souls of our fellow-men who are on the brink of endless ruin, and see it not."[38]

Relevance for today. Allow me now to list briefly what I consider the most important points for reconsideration in light of our own calling as evangelists today.

Grace is vital for preaching. Time spent in prayer and meditation is time well invested. We must depend upon God.

Inactivity breeds temptation. We must be employed in the work of the gospel, not only for the sake of those to whom God has called us to serve, but for our own sake as well.

Holy boldness tempered with loving concern for those around us is vital.

In closing, Asbury believed in the absolute uniqueness of our faith in Jesus Christ. That is not to say that we are right and the world is wrong. It is simply to say that this is what we believe and this is what motivates us for the Christian ministry. It is good to remember that those of us who hold to such a commitment today stand on giant shoulders.

Chapter 5: Baltimore, 1784

> They are now at full liberty simply to follow the Scriptures and the
> Primitive Church. And we judge it best that they should stand fast
> in that liberty wherewith God has so strangely made them free.

John Wesley's Letters

A society of people called Methodists, led by the lay preacher/
evangelist was about to become a church—the Methodist Episcopal
Church. This is how it happened.

Like John Wesley's Aldersgate experience, the Christmas Conference
in Baltimore was more than just a single event. It was a beginning and
an end. It was an end to a whole host of happenings brought to a climax
by the War for Independence. It was a beginning of a church, now
prepared to serve its people freely within that newly formed Union of
States. For this reason this founding conference serves as a pivotal
point, not only for the book as a whole, but for this chapter in
particular. Let us examine this important period in the movement
called Methodism with particular reference to its effect upon the evangelist. We will focus on the following headings: Thomas Coke, the
documents, the Christmas Conference, the immediate results, and
relevance for today.

Thomas Coke. In February 1784, Wesley called Coke into his private
quarters in order to reveal his plan for America. After reviewing the
necessity for action to be taken and then justifying his own right to take
such an action, Wesley asked Coke to accept ordination as superintendent for the Societies in the United States. Coke was reportedly startled
at first and questioned Wesley's authority to make such an appointment. Wesley, however, was a wise man. He knew that Coke's ambition
would soon outweigh his reticence. Accordingly, two months had
scarcely passed before Coke wrote to Wesley "informing him, that his
objections were silenced, and that he was ready to co-operate with him
in any way that was calculated to promote the glory of God, and the
good of souls."[1]

Wesley had reached an impasse. He was still determined that lay
preachers should not serve the sacraments. If Methodism was to

survive, therefore, he felt compelled to ordain one who could then ordain others in America. Whitehead records this letter from Coke to Wesley: "The more maturely I consider the subject, the more expedient it appears to me, *that the power of ordaining others should be received by me from you,* . . . I *may* want all the influence in America, which you can throw into my scale."[2] Then Coke makes an interesting observation regarding Asbury:

Mr. *Brackenbury* informed me at *Leeds*, that he saw a letter in *London* from Mr. *Asbury*, in which he observed, that he would not receive any person deputed by you with any part of the superintendency of the work invested in him: or words which evidently implied so much. I do not find any, the least degree of prejudice in my mind against Mr. Asbury, on the contrary, a very great love and esteem; and am determined not to stir a finger without his consent, unless sheer necessity obliges me; but rather to lie at his feet in all things.[3]

Wesley's wisdom, therefore, extended not only to the selection of Coke, the educated, the ordained; but to the selection of Asbury, the workhorse, the evangelist. This Cokesbury connection is an interesting mix. Coke was undeniably ambitious. He wanted power to rule in America, not merely to ordain in cases of emergency (as was Wesley's intent).[4]

Yet, Coke was a gifted man. He carried the ordination from John Wesley himself. He provided the necessary transition. He was a gifted administrator. As for Mr. Asbury, he had paid his dues on the American scene. He had walked out the land. He would not allow his labors to be clogged by inordinate British intervention. Coke wanted things to happen quickly. Asbury was more reserved. He felt that people would support that which they had helped to create. They had to be informed. So, the stage is set for Coke and Asbury. Watch as these two forces come together. It will make you want to believe in God.

Coke arrived in America on November 3, 1784. This is his *Journal* entry for November 14:

In this chapel (Barratt's Chapel) in the midst of a forest, I had a noble congregation, to whom I endeavored to set forth the Redeemer as our wisdom, righteousness, sanctification, and redemption. After the sermon, a plain, robust man came up to me in the pulpit and kissed me. I thought it could be no other than Mr. Asbury, and I was not deceived. I administered the sacrament, after preaching, to five or six hundred communicants, and held a love-feast. It was the best season I ever knew, except one at Charlemont in Ireland. After dinner Mr. Asbury and I had a private conversation on the future management of our affairs in America. He informed me that he had received some intimations of my arrival on the continent, and had collected a considerable number of the preachers to form a council, and if they were of opinion that it would be expedient immediately to call a Conference, it should be done. They were accordingly sent for, and after debate, were unanimously of that opinion. We therefore sent off Freeborn Garrettson, like an arrow, from north to south, directing him to send messages to the right and left, and to gather all the preachers together at Baltimore on Christmas-eve. Mr. Asbury has also drawn up for me a route of about a 1,000 miles in the meantime. He has given me his black (Harry by name), and borrowed an excellent horse for me. I exceedingly reverence Mr. Asbury; he has so much of wisdom and consideration, so much meekness and love; and under all this, though hardly to be perceived, so much command and authority. He and I had agreed to use our joint endeavors to establish a school or college. I baptized here thirty or forty infants, and seven adults. We had, indeed, a precious time at the baptism of the adults.[5]

It would be interesting to explore several of the references mentioned in that entry more closely. The college was a fiasco. The references to Black Harry and Freeborn Garrettson are significant. We will return to them in the next chapter. For now, it is important to note the genius of Wesley in bringing these two great men together. This was a solemn occasion. Accordingly, November 26 was set aside as a day of prayer and fasting that I (says Asbury) "might know the will of God in the matter that is shortly to come before our Conference; the preachers and people seem to be much pleased with the projected plan; I myself am led to think it is of the Lord. I am not tickled with the honor to be gained; I see danger in that way. My soul waits upon God. Oh, that he may lead us in the way we should go!"[6]

If the Methodists were to proceed in establishing a church, they needed guidelines. When Coke, Vasey, and Whatcoat arrived from England, they brought with them certain documents which would set the tone for the Conference itself. Let's look at them more closely.

The documents. Fredrick Norwood comments: "Considering his habit of arranging divine providences to suit himself, Wesley was in this case remarkably restrained. The Americans were not left without guidance and advice, but they were free to decide what they would do with them." [7] Let's look at this "guidance and advice." Coke, Vasey, and Whatcoat brought with them from Wesley at least three documents—Letters of Ordination, An Open Letter to the People in North America, and An Abridgement of the English Liturgy.

The Letters of Ordination were transcribed from the originals written in Wesley's own hand. The following is a copy and since it is not so well known, I give it to you in full:

To all to whom these presents shall come, John Wesley, late Fellow of Lincoln College, in Oxford, Presbyter of the Church of England, sendeth greeting.

Whereas many of the people in the southern provinces of North America, who desire to continue under my care and still adhere to the doctrines and discipline of the Church of England, are greatly distressed for want of ministers to administer the sacraments of baptism and the Lord's Supper, according to the usage of the said Church; and whereas there does not appear to be any other way of supplying them with ministers:

Know all men that I, John Wesley, think myself to be providentially called at this time, to set apart some persons for the work of the ministry in America. And therefore, under the protection of Almighty God, and with a single eye to his glory, I have this day set apart, as a superintendent, by the imposition of my hands and prayer (being assisted by other ordained ministers), Thomas Coke, Doctor of Civil Law, a Presbyter of the Church of England, and a man whom I judge to be well qualifed for that great work. And I do hereby recommend him to all whom it may concern as a fit person to preside over the flock of Christ. In testimony whereof, I have hereunto set my hand and seal this second day of September in the year of our Lord one thousand seven hundred and eighty-four. John Wesley.[8]

The open letter dated Bristol, September 10, 1784, is addressed "to *Dr. Coke, Mr. Asbury, and our brethren in North America.* It begins with Wesley's rationale for ordination. Then these words:

I have accordingly appointed Dr. Coke and Mr. Francis Asbury to be Joint Superintendents over our brethren in North America; as also Richard Whatcoat and Thomas Vasey to act as elders among them, by baptizing and administering the Lord's Supper. And I have pre-

46

pared a Liturgy little differing from that of the Church of England (I think, the best constituted National Church in the World), which I advised all the traveling preachers to use on the Lord's Day and all the congregations reading the Litany only on Wednesdays and Fridays and praying extempore on all other days. I also advised the elders to administer the Supper of the Lord on every Lord's Day." [9]

It continues with a statement regarding his failure at attempts to secure ordination by more conventional means. He then concludes:

As our American brethren are now totally disentangled both from the State and from the English hierarchy, we dare not entangle them again either with the one or the other. They are now at full liberty simply to follow the Scriptures and the Primitive Church. And we judge it best that they should stand fast in that liberty wherewith God has so strangely made them free. [10]

The liturgy mentioned in that letter was entitled *The Sunday Service of the Methodists in North America with Other Occasional Services,* commonly called *The Sunday Service* of 1784. This was printed by Wesley to be distributed by Coke. Besides containing the "Sunday Service," it contained "The Form and Manner of Making and Ordaining of Superintendents,[11] Elders, and Deacons." These were the three distinct offices of the ministry in an episcopally constituted church. Admittedly, the term *superintendent* replaced *Bishop* and the term *Elder* replaced *Presbyter* or *Priest,* but the services and the relative duties are the same as those for Bishop, Priest, and Deacon found in *The Book of Common Prayer,* 1662. It also included forms for the administration of baptism, the Lord's Supper, marriage, and burial. Interestingly enough, the only omission was a form for admission into membership or confirmation. That perhaps would have been too much to expect from the old man. His bias toward a sacramental approach for membership in the church within a parish system was too strong.

So, these three documents in addition to an abridged Articles of Religion (taken from the 39 Articles of the Church of England) and the Large Minutes gave those planning the conference enough "guidance and advice" to proceed with an agenda for their conference. These documents were studied carefully in mid-December at Perry Hall, a house outside Baltimore. Coke reported that it was "reckoned one of the most elegant in the thirteen states." He writes: "Here I have a noble room to myself, where Mr. Asbury and I may, in the course of a week, mature every thing for the Conference."

The Christmas Conference. Freeborn Garrettson did his job well. In less than six weeks, he rode throughout most of the country summoning the preachers/evangelists to the conference. The conference conceived in Barrett Chapel, planned in Perry Hall, was now ready to begin in Lovely Lane Meeting House in downtown Baltimore. The time had come. The documents were in hand. All that was needed was the consensus of those present that God wanted them in fact to form a body called the Methodist Episcopal Church. Over 60 of the 83 traveling preachers/evangelists were there.[12]

Lovely Lane Meeting House was a small stone structure built ten years earlier. It was 10:00 A.M., Friday, December 24. The conference opened. These are the events that followed.

Coke took the chair and read Wesley's open letter. Asbury wisely refused ordination to the superintendency unless so elected by the brethren. He was elected unanimously and so instituted a constitutional government more compatible with the American taste for democracy. Asbury was ordained deacon on Christmas Day by Coke and assisted by Vasey and Whatcoat. On the two days following, he was ordained Elder and Superintendent. His consecration to the superintendency was assisted by his friend, Philip Otterbein, a German Reformed pastor who figures prominently in Part III.

The remainder of the ten-day conference was left to the task of ordaining deacons and elders and organizing. Approximately three of the preachers/evangelists were ordained Deacon and twelve were ordained Elder (the exact number is uncertain). Coke preached the ordination sermon. It caused a considerable stir in England. Small wonder, when we read some of the lines taken from it:

You may not perceive the dreadful effects of raising immoral or unconverted men to the government of the Church. The baneful influence of their example is so extensive that the skill and cruelty of devils can hardly fabricate a greater curse than an irreligious bishop. But thou, O man of God, follow after righteousness, godliness, patience, and meekness. Be an example to the believers in word, in conversation, in charity, in spirit, in faith, in purity.[13]

The men ordained were an interesting lot. Our "founding fathers" were young, energetic, inexperienced in matters of church polity, but

48

wholly committed to God. One observed: "Perhaps such a number of holy, zealous, godly men never before met together in Maryland, perhaps not on the continent of America."[14]

From the ordinations the move was then to approve Wesley's general plan. The standards of doctrine received by British Methodism and named in the Deed of Declaration—Wesley's *Standard Sermons*, the *Notes on the New Testament*—were added to by the abridged Articles of Religion (reduced to twenty-four with the addition of one on "Civil Rulers," numbered 23, making twenty-five in all), the abridged Sunday Service and the "General Rules." All of these were approved unanimously, causing one to comment: "The secret of their success was their oneness of spirit. Like the disciples in the chamber at Jerusalem, 'they were all of one heart and one mind.' Whoever looks at the system of rules or of government devised and sent forth by the General Conference of 1784, must concede to it a 'wholesideness,' and unselfishness both as it regards the preachers themselves and the people under their care."[15]

Before moving on to the next section, let us look briefly at a few of the rules which relate to the evangelist. Rules were established, for example, regarding the conduct of preachers. Their responsibilities were outlined in some detail. They were to preach, to visit, to instruct the children, to study, but most of all their greatest ministry was to save souls. In order to save souls, the evangelist would have to travel. I am reminded of the words of Wesley regarding the itinerancy of his preachers:

Be their talents ever so great, they will, erelong, grow dead themselves, and so will most of those that hear them. I know, were I myself to preach one whole year in one place, I should preach both myself and most of my congregation asleep. Nor can I ever believe it was ever the will of our Lord that any congregation should have one teacher only. We have found, by long and constant experience, that a frequent change of teachers is best. This preacher has one talent, that another. No one, whom I ever knew, has all the talents which are needful for beginning, continuing, and perfecting the work of grace in the whole congregation.[16]

One more rule is particularly interesting in that it went against Wesley's plan.

No person could be ordained a superintendent, elder or deacon without the consent of a majority of the Conference and the consent and imposition of the hands of a superintendent. The superintendent was made amenable for his conduct to the Conference, "who had power to expel him for improper conduct if they see it necessary." If by death, expulsion, or otherwise, there be no superintendent remaining in our Church, "the Conference shall elect one, and the elders, or any three of them, shall ordain him according to our liturgy." [17]

Coke yelded to this "democratic form" but later regretted it when several of Wesley's nominees fr the episcopacy were rejected by the American brethren.[18]

By January 1 the business of the Conference had progressed to the place where they could discuss the establishmet of a college. It was to be called Cokesbury College and it was to be located at Abingdon, Maryland. The history of that college is a story unto itself. We must move on. On January 2 the Conference adjourned. These words from Asbury are perhaps a fitting summary: "We spent the whole week in Conference, debating freely, and determining all things by a majority of votes. The Doctor preached every day at noon and someone of the other preachers morning and evening. We were in great haste, and did much business in a little time." [19]

The immediate results. To say that the Methodist Episcopal Church was off and running would be an understatement. Bishop McTyeire writes, "The work of Church extension began at the Christmas Conference. Asbury took horse the day after adjournment and rode 40 miles. Lambert left for Antigua. Garrettson and Cromwell embarked for Nova Scotia, in view of which they had been ordained, about the middle of February; a voyage at that season, uncomfortable and even dangerous." [20] So, the Methodists scattered; they scattered to preach.

The preachers/evangelists were ordained. Although the preacher was now pastor, the pastor's first calling was to preach. The expansion of Methodism was not dependent upon preacher as pastor so much as it was upon preacher as evangelist. This is not to disparage of pastoring. Preaching was simply the primary instrument for spreading scriptural holiness throughout the land. And spread they did. Between 1784 and 1840, the Methodists grew from 18,000 to 580,000.

Although immediately after the Christmas Conference, the Societies still referred to themselves as Societies, this was due more to habit than to anything else. Admittedly, there was still little form of church government as such. No subsequent conference had been called upon the close of the Christmas Conference. Yet, the Methodist Episcopal Church was a reality. The preacher/evangelist was no longer without credentials to support his calling.

Norwood tends to play down the significance of the Baltimore Conference. He states that, apart from the historical context, the Conference was a date and nothing more. That is of course true, but this would be the case in almost any instance. The historical context is always important. Nonetheless, we cannot allow the events of this great conference to go unheralded. We cannot diminish the struggle, hard fought, to establish a body independent of all others. Methodism was alive. It was important. Its preachers/evangelists would carry its banners proudly.

Relevance for today. Most scholars agree that the Christmas Conference was called specifically to ordain preachers. Ordination, however, simply provided the preacher/evangelist with credentials necessary to fulfill all of the pastoral offices. Nothing else changed. Preaching was the key. The Methodist evangelist was first a preacher. Preaching has well nigh lost its appeal in many circles in recent years. "How are they to hear without a preacher?" (Rom. 10:14).

All of us, as United Methodists, have cause to be proud. Our church was started by holy men seeking the will of God for a needy people. The message was solid. The leadership had vision. The evangelists would in just fifty years make Methodism the religion of America.

A question: Is there hope for a renewal in United Methodism? Perhaps. The price is always great. Some will have to be willing to sacrifice all for the good of the kingdom. God's grace is available for the servant. Who among us will take towel in hand and wash the feet of a people increasingly difficult to reach? It frightens me to realize just how serious this business of preaching the gospel of Jesus Christ really is.

Again, the relevance for today is that we stand on giant shoulders. The characteristics of those newly ordained evangelists leaving Baltimore in January 1785 should lift the spirit and challenge the mind. Lord, do it again!

Chapter 6: Nothin' Out but Crows and Methodist Preachers

> There is one thing about that early itinerancy which should not be overlooked. It was as merciless a calling as ever challenged brave men. We have spoken of mobs, of jails, of long rides through the rain, of nights in the open, of days in the malaria-soaked swamps of the new frontier. "How did they ever stand it?" someone asked. The answer is that they didn't stand it. They died under it.
>
> Halford Luccock

If I were selling life insurance in the late eighteenth century, I would rather have insured bear wrestlers than Methodist preachers. The evangelists of the newly formed Methodist Episcopal Church rode hard, preached long, and died young. Their motto might well have been: "No pain, no reign!" Let me explain.

The Circuit Rider. By the time George Washington took office in 1789, there were no more than ten city churches that had what might be referred to as established congregations. The early Methodist preachers/evangelists were appointed to circuits, some of them as large as states. They preached in societies. They preached en route between societies—in taverns, inns, barnyards, jails, courthouses, or just a clearing in the woods. Any place was sufficient as long as it would support a "crowd" of five or ten hearers.

Of the circuit riders who died before 1847, nearly half died before the age of thirty. Two-thirds died before twelve years of service, and half of those before five years of service. If it is true that we will be heard with authority to the precise degree that we are willing to put our lives on the line, it is little wonder that the Methodist evangelists lit revival fires across the country that brightened the skies for thousands of miles.

The message of the circuit rider, on the whole, was true to Methodism. There were few moral harangues. The intent of preaching was to awaken, convert, and sanctify. They proclaimed to all that our very nature is out of orbit with God and apart from grace we are slave to sin, powerless to overcome those things that would diminish life. These evangelists insisted that grace was revealed only in Jesus Christ. Faith

53

in him and in him alone brought us to life eternal. Furthermore, life eternal, by necessity, led to perfection and good works as the inevitable fruit (though never the cause) of saving grace.

These circuit riders were not all out of the same mold. Some, like Benjamin Abbott, were uneducated. Others, like Philip Gatch, had a fair education according to the standards of the day. Some were married, but most (for obvious reasons) were single. A few were independently wealthy, but most had little or nothing, with no prospect for anything more. The annual salary grew during Asbury's tenure to $100 for bishops, elders, and deacons alike, but was rarely paid in full. When the Bishop read the appointments, it is said that the circuit rider on average could pack his saddle bags in five minutes and be on his way to a new circuit in ten. Often they would be sent to a circuit with no housing available. They would simply move into an area with the prospect that "once along the river, between this place and that, there was a family who, it was said, might have been open to the Methodists sometime past." Once the family was located and if the door was opened, hospitality was accepted, the family altar rededicated, prayers said, people gathered, a sermon preached, a society or class organized, and the next day the road to another perspective family was taken. The particular genius of the circuit evangelist was his ability to mix with the common folk because he was common folk himself.

The annals of early Methodist history in America are packed with remarkable stories concerning these circuit evangelists. Robert Southey devotes several pages to Benjamin Abbott and characterizes him as near insanity.[1] To be sure, Abbott's style was extreme, even for his day, but it was true to Abbott and to his particular call as a man of God. He followed his own leading, constantly looking for an opportunity to speak a word for God. I recall one account where he was asked to speak a word following a funeral sermon preached by an Anglican priest. As Abbott rose to speak, a thunderstorm broke. Seeing this (no doubt a sign from God) as an opportunity to increase his effect, he described the return of Christ at the Last Judgment. The thunder and lightning set a frightening pace. The thunder shook the building and the preaching shook the people. As he described the judgment upon the ungodly, he cried out: "It may be that he will descend in the next clap of thunder!" People began to scream and begged God for mercy, and as the storm slowly passed Abbott offered Jesus Christ as refuge from all their fears. When Abbott rode that circuit again fourteen years later, he remarks that he found twelve living witnesses who were converted during that sermon. Southey remarks that it had been argued that such preaching came from and led to insanity. Tell me. Is that madness or the finger of God? You be the judge. My mind is already made up. Admittedly, such methods might not work today or even in England during the same period, but this was the American frontier. People were tough and had generally desensitized themselves to pain, physical or spiritual. It took strong preaching to penetrate, and once the wound had been lanced, it bled freely for the moment and then quickly healed. No self-respecting frontiersman would weep in public. The one exception was during times of church revival. So, the emotions released at the mourner's bench of the circuit evangelist were unpacking additional baggage as well. This served to heighten the response. Not to worry. People's lives were still changed for the good. I am grateful for the instrument, no matter how crude or unconventional. I sometimes tell my students that good theology is not always an effective evangelistic tool. God will sometimes use the strangest "stuff" to get people saved.

If we are to look at the circuit evangelist in any detail, time and space force us to select a few representatives. Admittedly it is difficult to find a "typical" circuit evangelist, so I have chosen three in hopes of demonstrating much of what it must have been like for the rest of them—Freeborn Garrettson, Jesse Lee, and Harry Hosier. These were men well worth knowing.

Freeborn Garrettson. Like most circuit evangelists, Garrettson was American born. We have already glimpsed him riding "like an arrow" to announce a Christmas Conference in 1784. He grew up in Maryland and was converted under the Methodist preaching of men like Strawbridge, Asbury, and Shadford. His testimony is nearly predictable of early Methodists. Convinced of sin, he struggled against the time when he would give his life wholly to God, and when that time came he held nothing back, embracing not only the Savior, but His call to the Methodist itinerancy.

Garrettson itinerated in the South during the war years. Like some Methodists he refused to bear arms, and like most Methodists he was accused of being a British sympathizer, mobbed, beaten, fired upon, and eventually jailed. Asbury writes for March 17, 1780:

I rode to Johnstown, and from thence to William Law's; met Freeborn Garrettson, who came out of jail by order of the governor and council of Maryland, who had sent to the Governor of Delaware to know if Freeborn Garrettson were not a fugitive, and had received satisfactory information. Brother Garrettson preached on Matthew

55

xxv, 10: "And they that were ready went in with him to the marriage, and the door was shut." [2]

Garrettson liked that kind of text. Here is an account from his own *Journal* for 1979: "I visited Shepherd's Town [on the Frederick circuit in Virginia] lying high in the Potomac River. On the Lord's day, I attended the church [Anglican] and heard the minister preach on 'Keep Holy the Sabbath Day.'" [3] The sermon lasted but fifteen minutes and nothing was said about "the fall of man, faith or repentance." No doubt wishing to take up the slack, when the minister had finished, Garrettson asked if he could speak. Permission was then given and he announced a text: "How shall we escape if we neglect so great salvation?" The minister's response to Garrettson's remarks when asked by one of the congregation what he thought of this doctrine was: "He seems to bring scripture to prove it; it may be so, but if it is, I know nothing of it." [4]

Garrettson's early ministry was in Maryland, Virginia, both Carolinas, Pennsylvania, Delaware, and New Jersey. Eventually he extended as far as Nova Scotia, where he developed quite a reputation as a preacher. News of Garrettson's success reached Wesley, who nominated him for the superintendency, but for some reason the American conference refused to elect him. Not to be undone, Garrettson went immediately back to Maryland and worked all the harder, continuing in the itinerancy for fifty years. Eventually he went to New York, an area previously untouched by the Methodists. He writes:

I gave myself to earnest prayer for direction. I knew that the Lord was with me. In the night season, in a dream, it seemed as if the whole country up the North river, as far as Lake Champlain, east and west, was open to my view. After the Conference adjourned, I requested the young men to meet me. Light seemed so reflected on my path that I gave them directions where to begin, and which way to form their circuits. [5]

In two years, the territory between New York City to the Canadian border and westward to Niagara had been thoroughly aroused and many Methodists had been secured for Societies and classes.

When Garrettson had been in the ministry for fifty years (in light of the circumstances, that in itself was a miracle), he was called on to preach a special sermon before the New York Conference. He stated:

56

I traversed the mountains and valleys, frequently on foot, with my knapsack on my back, guided by Indian paths in the wilderness, when it was not expedient to take a horse, I had often to wade through morasses, half-leg deep in mud and water; frequently satisfying my hunger with a piece of bread and pork from my knapsack, quenching my thirst from a brook, and resting my weary limbs on the leaves of the trees. Thanks be to God! he compensated me for all my toils; for many precious souls were awakened and converted to God.[6]

Before moving on to Jessee Lee, one more thing needs to be said about Freeborn Garrettson. Lest you think these early Methodist preachers had no social conscience, give careful attention to the following. Not long after his ordination, Garrettson inherited his father's estate, including a number of slaves. He had always been impressed by them, and made a point to adapt his preaching for them alone. Slowly, however, he developed a sensitivity to their plight and soon felt the effects of his preaching grow feeble. He called his whole family together for a season of common prayer. Suddenly he heard the voice within saying: "It is not right for you to keep your fellow creatures in bondage; you must let the oppressed go free." Without a moment's hesitation, Garrettson freed these slaves, one and all. The effect? Listen to this:

I was now at liberty to proceed in worship. After singing, I kneeled to pray. Had I the tongue of an angel, I could not fully describe what I felt: all my dejection, all that melancholy gloom which preyed upon me, vanished in a moment, and a divine sweetness ran through my whole frame.[7]

Jesse Lee. It is said that Jesse Lee was even more of an evangelist than Garrettson. Like Garrettson, he too was native born, he refused to bear arms, and was eventually jailed. While still under arrest he began preaching, first to his guard and then to a crowd of soldiers. A revival broke out among the troops. The colonel begged him to reconsider his decision not to bear arms, as he did not wish to detain such a man, but Lee was adamant. Finally, he agreed to drive the regiment's baggage-wagon and was discharged four months later.

I like the story of Lee's "calling" to the itinerancy. At the Conference of 1782, Asbury saw Lee standing with a number of preachers between sessions. Asbury shouted: "I am going to enlist Brother Lee!" Quickly seizing the army metaphor, another responded: "What bounty do you give?" Asbury replied, "Grace here and glory hereafter will be given him if he is faithful." So, Jesse Lee (over 250 pounds of him) entered the Methodist itinerancy.

Lee is perhaps best known for his opening of New England to Methodism. At the close of the conference held in New York, May 1789, the appointment was read: "Stamford—Jesse Lee." Stamford was the first town in Connecticut, so this circuit in effect meant that Lee had the whole of New England where there was not a single Methodist and the Methodists' reputation had long been dismissed as fanaticism and heresy. Lee left immediately and was frequently rebuffed. On a cold wintry Christmas Eve he writes:

> To-night, thanks be to God, I was invited by a widow woman to put up at her house. This is the first invitation I have had since I first came to the place, which is between six and seven months. O my Lord, send more laborers into this part of thy vineyard! I love to break up new ground, and hunt the lost souls in New England, though it is hard work; but when Christ is with me, hard things are made easy and rough waves made smooth.[8]

Still, the rough waves continued for some years. It was over a year before five circuits were mapped out with nearly 200 members. The "religion" of egalitarian democracy was a tough nut to crack. It has long been said that the Unitarians believed in the fatherhood of God, the brotherhood of man, and the neighborhood of Boston. Nonetheless, by 1792 a New England Methodist Conference had been organized with 481 members. That is no small miracle.

Lee was not an educated man as such. His formal training was limited. Nonetheless, he was quick to defend his calling. Bishop McTyeire gives this interesting description of Lee:

> Ready and witty when self-defense called for it, he was also loving and pathetic: at once tender and sharp, the very man for such an enterprise. He possessed a courage which nothing could daunt, and a cheerfulness that never failed. His style of address was full of shrewdness as well as of force, whereby he could rivet the attention of any audience, going straight to the hearts of his hearers, "putting them at once on the defensive if they were inclined to controversy, or carrying them completely with him if they were honest seekers after the truth." In person of magnificent presence, thirty-two years old and above the ordinary size, he had the manners of a Christian

gentleman, and could sing the Methodist hymns in a style that left little use for church-bells to call together his congregation. His crowning endowment for a mission among the descendants of the Puritans was an abiding conviction that he was directed by God to bestow on them some spiritual gifts which they needed. Full of the Holy Ghost and faith he did not expect a holiday recreation; he counted on difficulties and discouragements, but he had faith in the power of the gospel. It was the old battle of lamps and pitchers, of the sword of the Lord and of Gideon.[9]

At times, Lee was equally as quick to defend his education as he was his calling. Once when a minister sought to embarrass him by questioning him in Latin, Lee quickly replied in German (bits he had picked up while in ministry in North Carolina). This greatly surprised the minister, so that he repeated his question in Greek. Lee once again replied in German. The minister, not understanding German (thinking no doubt that it was Hebrew), concluded that Lee knew more than he himself and that he could preach in his church. Somehow there is justice in that story. Lee died in the same year that Asbury died. Here is a report of his last sermon.

There is something peculiarly touching in delivering the last sermon. At a camp-meeting near Hillsborough, on the eastern shore of Maryland, on Saturday afternoon, 22d of August, 1816, Mr. Lee preached his last sermon from a favorite text: "but grow in grace." 2 Peter iii, 18. It is said, that when he gave out the text it was in this singular manner; "you may find my text in the *last* epistle of Peter, the last chapter of the *last* verse; and I know not but I am to preach my *last* sermon." It was his last message to a lost world. The sermon was powerful and efficient, worthy of the last effort of one who was standing upon the walls of Zion for the last time.[10]

Harry Hosier. Harry Hosier was the first black local preacher among the Methodists. Booker T. Washington claims that he was the first black preacher in the United States.[11] "Black Harry," as he was known, was a remarkable man.

Black Harry and Richard Allen were the only two blacks at the Christmas Conference. Born a slave near Fayetteville, North Carolina, he was converted and freed when Asbury first met him. He was illiterate and refused to learn how to read (although Richard Allen offered to teach him) for fear that it would hamper his freedom in preaching.

He was a frequent traveling companion for Asbury, Coke, Whatcoat, and Garrettson. Asbury's plan was for Hosier to preach to the blacks, and oh, how the man could preach. Coke writes:

> Monday 29, I preached at one *John Purnell's*. I have now had the pleasure of hearing *Harry* preach several times. I sometimes give notice immediately after preaching, that in a little time *Harry* will preach to the blacks; but the whites always stay to hear him. Sometimes I publish him to preach at candle-light as the Negroes can better attend at that time. I really believe he is one of the best preachers in the world, there is such an amazing power attends his preaching, though he cannot read; and he is one of the humblest creatures I ever saw.[12]

Many shared Coke's high opinion of Harry Hosier. He was regarded as one of the foremost Methodist preachers. He was eloquent when expressing God's redeeming grace. He could recite long passages taught to him by Asbury.

Hosier first appeared in Asbury's *Journal* in 1780 in North Carolina. Asbury writes: "I have thought if I had two horses and Harry (a coloured man) to go with, and drive one, and meet the black people, and to spend about six months in Virginia and the Carolinas, it would be attended with a blessing."[13]

We find him with Asbury again in Virginia preaching on the "barren fig tree." Asbury comments that "the whites looked on with attention."[14] Here, however, Asbury reports that "certain sectarians are greatly displeased with him because he tells them they may fall from grace, and that they must be holy."[15] Harry lived long enough to illustrate both of these truths with his own life. A few months after the previous incident, Asbury reports from Delaware, "Harry seems to be unwilling to go with me: I fear his speaking so much to white people in the city has been, or will be, injurious; he has been flattered and may be ruined."[16] Asbury's words proved prophetic. Shortly afterward, Harry took to the bottle and fell from grace only to be reclaimed sometime later for the rest of his life. By 1785 Harry Hosier was again traveling regularly with the Methodist greats.

In 1791 we find Hosier returning from Nova Scotia with Freeborn Garrettson. Asbury reports here that Hosier preached to congregations of more than a thousand. Hosier also helped to establish circuits in New England. In fact, the first mention of a Methodist preacher in any New York newspaper is of Harry (*New York Packet*, September 11, 1786).

Herbert Asbury writes appropriately of Harry Hosier:

> He was converted in the usual Methodist manner, with fits, convulsions, and terrible emotional and mental sufferings, but later wicked people corrupted him with a glass of wine and he became a backslider and a sinner. However, he prayed all night under a tree and again found saving grace, if not sanctification. He died in 1810 [in Philadelphia] and went to heaven."[17]

Harry Hosier, God bless him, was only the beginning, however, for blacks among the Methodists. By the time of Emancipation, Southern Methodism showed thousands of black preachers, exhorters, and class leaders, who could read their Bibles and edify their congregations.

Discipline. Before moving on to other important matters, a word needs to be said here about American Methodism's system of disciplining its preachers/evangelists. Although the distances were great and Wesley was not there to question them personally, the ranks among early Methodist preachers/evangelists were kept surprisingly clean. Any breach of conduct was cause for suspension. The stakes were too high to risk the finger of scorn.

Discipline still worked within the connection. Although not as tightly drawn as in British Methodism under Wesley, the Conference watched its preachers carefully. Bishops, elders, deacons, all took the rules of their church seriously and held each other accountable with the love of a brother and the threat of expulsion.

Relevance for today. Times have changed. In light of those changes and in light of the "itinerancy" today, many traveling evangelists are closer to the roots of Methodism than the man or woman serving the local church. Is traveling evangelism still a legitimate call? That is a fair question, but the answer should be heard with authority. Until the local church reaches into every person's world with the presentation of the gospel message, *you bet it is*! Until all Christians understand their call to ministry within their own sphere of influence, the traveling evangelist will take up the slack. Until the church as a whole acknowledges its calling to evangelize all those within reach, the evangelist will travel the highways and biways calling the lost to salvation in Jesus Christ.

One last point needs to be emphasized. Timothy L. Smith's book, *Revivalism and Social Reform,* makes the point that the social gospel is actually an outgrowth from, not a reaction against, revivalism. During the 1840s, for example, the cry of the Finney Revival was "repent, believe, and become an abolitionist!"

The lives of the early circuit evangelists demonstrate this balance between the social gospel and the personal gospel beautifully. May we take heart and endeavor once again to follow them as they followed Jesus. Giant shoulders carry crosses frequently in the form of another person's burden. The call of the gospel, evangelical or otherwise, is a call against sin—individual and corporate. May we learn our lesson well.

Part III
The United Brethren and Evangelical Association

Chapter 7:
The Otterbein/Albright Models

After I had experienced the grace of regeneration, I soon recognized the fact that the surest and best way to work out my soul's salvation, and to be ready at all times to fight the good fight of faith was, to be in fellowship with devout Christians, and to take part in bearing the cross, to pray for and with one another, to be vigilant and edify each other by means of an exemplary life in the service of God.

Jacob Albright (from his autobiography)

The *United* side of United Methodism makes considerable contribution to the history, role, and influence of the evangelist in the movement called Methodism. The connections between the United Brethren and Evangelical Association (Evangelical United Brethren after 1946) and Methodism are many and varied long before union in 1968. Both Otterbein and Albright had close association with Methodism in America from the beginning. Yet, the Evangelical United Brethren influence is unique. The EUB legacy is far more involved than we sometimes acknowledge. The EUB's were far more than Methodists with German accents. Their roots link with the European continental reformers which (in some respects) Wesley and Asbury nearly missed altogether. *United* Methodism connects with Luther and Calvin as well as with Cranmer, Ridley, and Latimer. Yet, in spite of their strong Reformed ties, the moderate pietism of Otterbein and Albright made them compatible with the theology and polity of American Methodism. It is a fascinating story. Let's get started.

Although their stories will be told more or less separately, we have selected both Otterbein and Albright as models partly because of their personal contrasts (paralleling Wesley and Asbury in many ways) but primarily because of their influence within their own movements as extraordinary evangelists who bring something special and unique to the interesting mix called United Methodism. Although the material here will be somewhat abbreviated due to our dual task, the format for the modeling chapters remains the same for both men.

Otterbein and Albright provide unusual contrast for men with so much in common. Otterbein was highly educated while Albright was virtually self-taught. Their backgrounds, places of birth, styles of ministry, differ greatly, yet their movements surfaced within three years of each other in close proximity and with similar (if not identical) goals. Let's meet them.

PHILIP WILLIAM OTTERBEIN (1726-1813)

Introduction. William Otterbein (the name Philip was rarely used) was born in Dillenburg, Germany. Dillenburg, the capital of the State of Nassau, was a town of about 3,000 people. William's father, John Daniel, was a minister in the German Reformed Church until his early death in 1742. William was but sixteen. William's mother, Henrietta, a devoutly pious woman, raised her six boys and one girl and saw personally that all of her six sons graduated from the Herborn Theological Academy. Herborn was an academy with university status located in the town of Herborn, three miles south of Dillenburg. It was a school of the German Reformed Church and held to the Calvinistic tradition as modified or softened by the moderate theology of the Heidelberg Catechism. It was a major center of Pietism in the Reformed Church. William and all five of his brothers became pastors in the Reformed Church. His only sister married a Reformed pastor.

After graduation, Otterbein served as a private tutor for some months before returning to Herborn where he was an instructor in the biblical languages while completing his theological training. In 1749 he was ordained and became pastor in Ockersdorf where he quickly organized Bible studies and prayer meetings (after the order of the *collegia pietatis*). This aroused considerable opposition among the nominal church leaders, but Otterbein persisted in his evangelical views and continued to minister there effectively for a number of years. Then in 1752 he responded to the missionary call from Michael Schlatter who, representing the Synodal headquarters in Amsterdam for the Reformed Church, was seeking recruits for the thousands of German immigrants who had fled religious persecution and were now in America.

Otterbein remained in America for the rest of his life (except for a visit to Germany in 1771). There he pastored the leading congregations of the Reformed Church. From 1752 until 1758 he pastored a church in

Lancaster, Pennsylvania. There he instituted a covenant for the spiritual discipline of members intending to receive the sacrament of the Lord's Supper. From 1758 to 1760 Otterbein was at Tulpehocken, Pennsylvania where he began the first stated prayer meetings in America. From 1760 to 1765 he was at Frederick, Maryland. During this pastorate he married Susanna LeRoy, but she died after only six years of marriage. Otterbein never remarried and they had no children. From 1765 to 1774 Otterbein pastored in York, Pennsylvania. Then in 1774 he left York for Baltimore where he remained until his death nearly forty years later.

In Baltimore, Otterbein pastored the New Evangelical Reformed Church (today the Old Otterbein United Methodist Church). The New Evangelical Reformed Church was more or less an independent church which maintained connection both with the Reformed Church and a budding fellowship of United Brethren. Otterbein and Martin Boehm had established this fellowship among the German pastors who kept their old church ties while seeking a higher fellowship in Christ to satisfy some of their pietistic convictions and mystical experiences. Raymond Albright writes: "By 1800 there was a sufficient nucleus for a definite organization among their followers and Otterbein and Boehm were elected to the office of 'Aeltesten' (literally 'elders,' but certainly meaning bishop or superintendent). Now they preached with as much zeal as before but with the added incentive of winning followers for their groups."[1] Otterbein, himself, had this dual relationship with the Reformed Church and the United Brethren in Christ throughout his life. Otterbein, in this Baltimore setting, established thimself as an evangelist throughout the area. He extended his ministry through frequent field tours, emerging as the leader of the evangelical wing of the Reformed Church and as the foremost American spiritual mentor to the younger Francis Asbury, whom (as we have observed) he helped to ordain in 1784. Interestingly enough, the confessions of faith and the church order for the Baltimore Church became the basis for the first United Brethren *Discipline* in 1815.

Message. While still in Germany, Otterbein quickly established a reputation for a style of preaching that was vigorous and direct. As for the content of his message, we know that he laid a great deal of stress on regeneration. Theologically, the definitive work of all of Otterbein's extant writings is a sermon entitled: "The Salvation-Bringing Incarnation and the Glorious Victory of Jesus Christ Over the Devil and Death."[2] Behney and Eller's monumental work *The History of the Evangelical United Brethren Church* summarizes this sermon in fifteen statements.[3] These statements include the classic themes of God as justice and mercy, judgment and love. Men and women are seen as too sinful to save themselves. Christ is depicted as God's incarnation intervening on our behalf. There is also a recurring emphasis upon the necessity of a broken and contrite heart on our part causing us to join with Christ in dying to sin through suffering. This identification with Christ leads to reconciliation through "Christ in us." Otterbein writes: "If there is no Christ in us, there is also no Christ for us. . . . We are children of wrath by nature, without God and without hope. Hence, Christ and his death do not profit us unless Christ comes inside us and destroys the kingdom of sin, penetrating us spirit, soul, and body with his light and life." [4]

Repeatedly there is an emphasis upon genuine repentance and conversion. Only the new creature in Christ is acceptable to God. Christ in us brings assurance, a change of heart, a renovation of spirit, and a victory over sin.

Sanctification also has repeated emphasis. Otterbein writes: "Whoever here fights under the discipline of the Holy Spirit is led to victory finally by grace. And this is the work of redemption, *Christ in us*. The marks by which it can be recognized are a loss of the desire or tendency toward sin, a ceasing of sin itself (Romans 6:6 and 18). The fruits of it are holiness (Romans 6:22), a new human being (Col. 3:10-14), and a process of life which goes on steadily toward perfection (2 Cor. 3:18)." [5] This last point ties in with both Wesley and Asbury as sanctification is seen as a process. I like these words from the sermon mentioned earlier: "Whoever clings to grace and stays close to Jesus, and whoever rushes to God with persistent faith-filled prayer will keep on going. Growth is a mark of the state of grace and stabilizes the heart." [6]

Again, consistent with both Wesley and Asbury (not to mention his Reformed pietism), Otterbein emphasizes the Bible over theology. In an outline for a sermon preached in 1802 he writes: "To be careful, and to preach no other doctrine than what is plainly laid down in the Bible." [7]

One final point is vital to Otterbein's message. Although a great deal of his preaching is consistent with his background in Reformed pietism, there is an obvious break with that tradition. One of the articles written for the church in Baltimore reads: "No preacher can stay among us who teacheth the doctrine of predestination, or the impossibility of falling from grace. . . ." [8] This particular stand against Calvinism caused Otterbein considerable trouble among some of his colleagues within the Reformed Church but also set the stage for the United Brethren Church soon to follow.

Character. While still in Germany, Otterbein quickly earned the reputation as a man of character. Read this testimonial from one of his professors:

> He [Otterbein] has always lived an honest, pious, and Christian life; and not only by much preaching and faithful declaring the Word of God in this city, as also at a near affiliating town, where he had been Vicar for a considerable time, and at other places but also by his godly life has built up the church. Wherefore we do not doubt that he will faithfully and fruitfully serve the church in Pennsylvania, to which he has been called.[9]

As far as I can tell, although Otterbein was a widower for most of his life there is not a whisper of scandal that relates either to life or ministry.

Style. Unlike both Wesley and Asbury, Otterbein worked from a congregational base. That is, he was primarily a pastor. Not that he was not an evangelist. He most certainly was. It is just that he was first a pastor evangelizing within the body and then constantly reaching out beyond, to the lost in his own and neighboring communities. He would frequently travel as much as 300 miles in a month. Once Otterbein left a parish, it would sometimes take two men to replace him.

We have already noted the evangelistic style of his preaching. The United Brethren historian Henry Spayth describes Otterbein's preaching as zealous and reformatory.[10] Otterbein's mother once stated: "My William will have to be a missionary; he is so frank, so open, so natural, so prophet-like."[11]

Christian Newcomer, a convert of Otterbein's and a pioneer figure in the early expansion of the United Brethren Church, describes Otterbein's preaching as "filled with energy and power. It had a plainness of language which some thought to be matchless."[12] In my own reading of Otterbein's works I was impressed with his ability to communicate, frequently charging his thoughts with short pithy statements like: "Beware," or "What a pity!" or "Listen to me," or "Notice!" Yet, there was a charm in his speaking which captured the listener. Listen to still another description: "Dignified in his deportment, in the pulpit, he spoke calmly, solemnly, and tenderly. His enunciation was distinct, and his thoughts ran in a clear and logical order, while his exhortations moved, with great power, the emotions of his audience."[13] So, from all of this it is clear that Otterbein's style was earnest, evangelical in tone, and deeply caring for others. He also had a heart for reaching out to those in need. His social consciousness has been well documented. Equally important was his emphasis upon evangelism *plus* nurture. Arthur Core in his classic little book on Otterbein writes:

In addition to evangelizing there must also be catechetical training of the young, nurture through Bible study and prayer groups to assure Christian growth and readiness for Christian service, general education for all people that they become literate and responsible citizens, and theological education to provide an indigenous leadership. His evangelical concern extended to all people and nothing should be spared to reach them with the gospel. His pastoral oversight comprehended the persons, the parish, the Coetus (the ruling body of the Reformed Church), and the mutual sharing of his own denomination. His total ministry did, indeed, reach "other places" and "build up the church." [14]

A final word about preaching and the importance of the classes before moving on to other matters. In previous chapters we have had opportunity to study the preacher or traveling evangelist. Here we have observed the pastor/evangelist. Otterbein is especially important as a transitional figure for many who rightly see themselves as "evangelists in residence." Here is a committed pastor who remained in a single parish for nearly four decades but who was nonetheless a powerful evangelist.

A word must also be spoken regarding Otterbein's emphasis upon the classes. Otterbein was forever organizing. Like Wesley and Asbury, he was concerned with backsliding. He knew full well that he needed to extend his own arms in order to sustain the flock. Consequently, he had the people look one to another. For example, when Otterbein went to Baltimore he did quickly what he had done in his previous pastorates. He established classes within the congregation, both for men and women. It was here that much of the work of renewal took place. It was here that the people were held accountable with regard to their own spiritual development. It was here that Christian growth took place so that sin was being "rooted out." Here perfection was not taught as an impossible ideal but as a very present reality for those who would take seriously the biblical mandates to press on toward the mark of their "high calling."

Motivation. Otterbein's primary motivation was a deep concern for people. His interest was not only spiritual but physical as well. He was concerned not only for the welfare of the people within his own church but within the larger community as well. There is much evidence for his having brought relief to individual families by gathering goods and distributing food and clothing to those in need.

As an evangelist Otterbein also had a deep concern for the spiritual well-being of those around him. He feared that his German neighbors (because of the language barrier or cultural differences) would somehow be lost to the gospel. Would they go to English-speaking churches? He feared not. So, Otterbein sought to stand in the gap for the German brethren and he enlisted others to do the same. Although his roots were not Wesleyan, as *United* Methodists, this great pastor/evangelist makes us all proud.

JACOB ALBRIGHT (1759-1808)

Introduction. Jacob Albright was born near Pottstown, Pennsylvania to German Lutheran immigrants. He was given the rudiments of a general education in German but learned to speak enough English to get by in communicating with his English neighbors. He was seventeen when the Revolutionary War broke out. Ludwig, his older brother, was killed in the war, and Jacob entered the Pennsylvania militia, serving at first as a drummer and then as a guard in a prison camp.

In 1785 Albright married Catherine Cope and bought a farm at Hahnstown, Pennsylvania. Albright's farm was fertile and productive. Catherine bore him six children but "several" died in an epidemic of dysentery in 1790. This loss came as a severe blow. By then Albright had also built a prosperous brick and tile business using the valuable limestone and clay deposits on his farm. Although he was an honest man, his religious experience within Lutheranism had not prepared him to cope with the loss of his children. He sought help elsewhere. First he went to Reverend Anthony Houtz, an evangelically minded German Reformed minister from Harrisburg who conducted the funeral services for his children. Next he went to Isaac Davies, a Methodist lay preacher from a neighboring farm. He then went to Adam Riegel, another neighbor and lay preacher associated with the fellowship of United Brethren begun by Otterbein and Boehm. After nearly losing his life in several farming accidents he began going daily to Riegel's home for instruction in the Christian faith. Together they spent hours in prayer. He writes:

This persevering and fervent prayer brought me nearer and nearer to my enlightenment. I realized power to consecrate myself to good

71

things, and to submit my will entirely to the will of God. I heard the voice of consolation in my soul; then I learned to understand and was convinced that since God does not desire the destruction of a sinner but that he should turn from his way and live, he would look upon my sincere penance and contrition of my heart with gracious eyes and that the merit of my Lord and his bitter suffering and death would complete the work.[15]

Complete the work he did. Conviction of sin turned to an assurance of salvation which led him to seek fellowship with a Methodist class meeting in the home of Davies where he eventually received an exhortor's license in 1796.

At first Albright was reluctant to preach but again an overwhelming conviction led him to itinerate as an evangelist. He already knew the Lutheran catechisms but now he sought to immerse himself in the scriptures as well. He also spent long periods of time in prayer and meditation.

As Albright continued to preach, he went further and further afield, forcing him to lose contact with the local Methodists as he was no longer able to attend their regular meetings. His evangelistic preaching, however, opened up new avenues for an ever-increasing and effective ministry.

Message. The content of Albright's preaching was similar in many ways to Otterbein's. Certainly Albright had plenty of opportunity to hear Otterbein as Otterbein preached throughout the area during Albright's most formative years. We can begin, therefore, by listing several of the themes that they held in common.

Apart from the fundamental themes of the Bible, both Albright and Otterbein emphasized the efficacy of suffering. We must identify with the suffering of Christ if we are to experience his resurrection.

Albright, like Otterbein, made continual reference to the experience of sanctification. The effects of the Methodist class meetings can also be seen upon Albright's understanding of sanctification. In fact, Albright might well have been even closer to Wesley on this important doctrine than was Otterbein. In words almost identical to Wesley's, Albright taught that, once converted, a person could be perfected through an experience of grace that was both instantaneous and gradual. It is gradual in the sense that one progresses to the moment of sanctification where one is made holy or pure in heart and mind. Again, as with Wesley, even the state of perfection must then be improved. Albright laid continual stress on the importance of striving constantly for further growth in grace.

Albright was not content that he should preach this doctrine alone. He insisted that all of his followers lay equal emphasis upon an experience of sanctification to be attained in this life. In fact, the emphasis was so strong that this became a point of contention between the early Evangelical Association and the early United Brethren.

Although Albright's message had distinctive characteristics, these doctrines were not taught in isolation. Behney and Eller provided us with a good summary of his basic religious emphases as such.

While he gave great emphasis to the doctrine of sanctification, it was only part of a well-rounded theological system. A summary of his religious emphases can be set forth in the following propositions: (1) The God of the Bible is the true God; (2) He sent Jesus Christ to save men; (3) men are helpless in their sins, and no self-righteousness or ritualistic ceremony can redeem them; (4) sinful men are not so completely separated from God but that they can repent and call upon God for salvation; (5) faith in Jesus Christ, the Son of God, will be answered by God's saving grace; (6) this is revealed in the cross of Christ; (7) one who is touched by this grace will live a godly or sanctified life; (8) sanctification is a promise which should be claimed by all saved men.[16]

So, Albright's message was inclusive, yet, in all honesty, there was an inflexibility about his style that caused many to take issue with his message. Albright not only knew what God had called him to preach, he also knew just how this message should reveal itself in the life of the believer. For example, he laid a great deal of stress on rigid morality. That brings us to our next heading.

Character. Albright's contacts with the Methodists not only influenced his message but to a high degree the content of a Christian lifestyle as well. This quotation from his autobiography quoted in Miller is especially revealing:

I strove to be temperant, and exercised myself much in fasting and prayer, which I always found to be the best means in the hour of trial, for I had very severe temptations and inward struggles, and when in a strait whether or not to heed the counsel of others, I continued more earnestly and constantly in prayer, which always helped me to overcome my enemies. However, I also found that the encouragement and advice of true, pious and experienced servants of God were a strong support. In this manner I became more mature in the knowledge of God; and by means of my struggle and trials, and the victory which the grace of God afforded me, my faith and determination to do good became firmer; and through persevering and fervent prayer, I realized constantly greater trust.[17]

Without question, Albright's life was consistent with his preaching. As is often the case, however, persons who are consistent with their own teaching will frequently insist upon that same kind of consistency among others. This was sometimes difficult to accept. Criticism of Albright's inflexibility was not limited to his antagonists. Even his own family had a difficult time adjusting. He once said: "It makes a person feel sad, to go out in the world to preach repentance and conversion, when one's family is yet unconverted, but I still have hope for my (daughter) Sarah."[18] Albright was also known to have grieved because of his son David's "intemperate life." Nevertheless, after Albright's death, his wife, Sarah, and David eventually became affiliated with the Evangelical Association.

Style. We already have several clues to Albright's style. Although his preaching was somewhat argumentative, his sermons were methodical and convincing. Bishop Orwig writes:

Mr. Albright's sermons were plain, — well adapted to the capacities of his hearers, and generally full of unction and irresistible power. His whole soul was in the work, and God enabled him to preach the Gospel with great freedom of speech. It often happened that his hearers were carried away by his sermons as by an irresistible torrent, and were so powerfully moved and affected, that many became convinced of their lost condition and repented; while the believers were always greatly edified and encouraged by his discourses. Opposition, slander, calumny, and persecution were, as a matter of course, not wanting; . . . Lukewarm and slothful nominal Christians, dead in trespasses and sins, read their sentence of condemnation in his sermons which reproved all injustice, sanctimoniousness and hypocrisy; and even well disposed Christians sometimes took offence at his unusual zeal in the cause of his Divine Master.[19]

In many ways Albright was an interesting mix. He was zealous, yet he constantly guarded against overemotionalism.[20] He warned against ceremony (especially when it smacked of hypocrisy), yet he was highly structured in his own spiritual discipline, and eventually the polity of the Evangelical Association would be more organized than that of the United Brethren.

Albright also laid a great deal of emphasis upon classes. As were Wesley, Asbury, and Otterbein, he too was especially concerned with backsliding. Consequently, he organized classes for the express purpose of nurturing young Christians. The classes served also as an opportunity of instruction for future leadership within the movement itself. Not surprisingly, several of the Albright people experienced their "calls to preach" in these early class meetings.

To summarize, one might say that Albright simply could not bear halfway measures. Those who insist on total commitment to Christ will always find persecution. To close this section on a more positive note, however, read these words taken from some of his earliest friends describing his overall style of ministry: "His forthright denunciation of sin and sinful men could sting hearers into reprisals. Yet this harshness did not really portray the man whose heart burned with love toward Christ and toward his neighbors for whom he wanted salvation. Those who understood him in this way regarded him as one whose face 'shown as it had been the face of an angel.' [21] This brings us to our next heading.

Motivation. Albright also had a deep burden for the lost. He had special concern for his German neighbors and agonized for their salvation. Albright, quite simply, preached because he felt he had to preach. The call was too sure and the burden too great. Let's close with his own words:

A burning love to God and all his children, and towards my fellow men generally, pervaded my being. Through this love, which the peace of God shed abroad in my heart, I came to see the great decline of true religion among the Germans in America, and felt their sad condition very keenly. I saw in all men, even in the deeply depraved, the creative hand of the Almighty. I recognized them as my brethren, and heartily desired that they might lead my German brethren into a knowledge of the truth, that he would send them true and exemplary teachers, who would preach the gospel in its power, in order to awaken the dead and slumbering religious professors out of their sleep of sin, and bring them again to the true life of godliness, so that they, too, might become partakers of the blessed peace with God and the fellowship of the saints in light. [22]

Relevance for today. This chapter is relevant for a number of reasons. First of all, Otterbein provides us with an excellent example of the evangelist within a local congregation. Never let it be said that the local pastor cannot be an evangelist as well.

Once again it is important to realize that the basic messages of both Otterbein and Albright conform to the classic doctrines of an evangelical faith. Both emphasized the primacy of scripture. Both emphasized repentance and conversion. Both understood suffering, and rather than being turned away by it allowed it to drive them even closer to the throne of grace. Both emphasized sanctification. It is interesting that even our continental roots focused on a doctrine that has become the hallmark of Methodism. Finally, both emphasized Christian nurture and established classes for the express purpose of sustaining those being converted by their preaching and the preaching of their followers. Here is an interesting paragraph from Frederick Norwood's *The Story of American Methodism*:

> Underlying the concept of the church in both of the forerunners of the Evangelical United Brethren is an idea strongly rooted in the pietism of the previous century: the *ecclesiola* in *ecclesia*, the little church within the church. Originally, this meant the nurture of small informal groups within the structure of the state church (Lutheran or Reformed in continental countries). Although formal membership remained in the official structure, spiritual fellowship was found in the small groups, the "little churches," within the great church (the established institution). In this way a dual membership existed; one formally in the state church, the other informally in the "society," the *Gemeinde* composed of those persons who *experienced* divine saving grace in their own lives and who were at least seeking to go on in perfect love and sanctification.[23]

Time and again our models seem to be reminding us of the importance of the classical evangelical themes along with the importance of Christian nurture as assured by small gatherings of Christians devised to turn struggling Christians into warriors for Christ and his kingdom.

Chapter 8: Unity in Christ

Wir sind Brüder! (We are brethren).
Otterbein's words spoken to Martin Boehm
at their first meeting in 1767

Frequently evangelists are portrayed as solitary people jealous of their independent status lest they be inhibited in their efforts to proclaim the gospel with prophetic utterance. No one likes prophets. Prophets stand alone against the world and are often portrayed as disdaining any connectional system, let alone ecumenism. Their words of warning and promise are often contrary to the prevailing winds of doctrine. Their demands are great. They require change, sometimes radical change, and change can be difficult to accept. Too easily we write them off as fanatics.

Much of the above, however, is only a stereotype—it is unfair, it is a lie. A different view of the evangelist can be seen in the beginnings of the United Brethren and Evangelical Association. Here unity is the key. There is a reason for this. Let's look closer.

Pietism. Both Otterbein and Albright were products of German pietism. A brief look at the emphases within pietism gives us an immediate clue as to the emphases within the early United Brethren and Evangelical Association. There can be little doubt that pietism created much of their vision.

The pietists in Germany were weary of controversy. The Thirty Years War (1618-1648) took a devastating toll on most Christian communities. In fact, the first stirrings of ecumenism can be traced to those attempts to regroup after what was essentially a religious war. Ecumenists like George Calixtus (1586-1656), Hugo Grotius (1586-1645), John Durie (1596-1680), and G. W. Leibnitz (1646-1716), were in a sense setting the stage for Philip Jacob Spener (1635-1705), the immediate source of pietism and August Hermann Franke (1663-1727), its leading educator and social reformer. Spener and Franke were grieved by the controversy over doctrine. Despairing of attempts to unite the church externally, they sought close fellowships internally with the establishment of small groups which were later expanded into the *collegia pietatis* (hence the name Pietism).

77

These small groups gathered first to discuss the Sunday sermons, pray, and study the Bible. Spener was concerned with the lack of spirituality among so-called Christians. Christianity had been reduced to believing right doctrines, receiving the sacraments, and attending the ordinances, with little or no reference to a personal relationship with Jesus Christ. Much of Christianity had little bearing on everyday living. Preaching in the churches was dry, formal, and sterile. In 1675 Spener published his *Pia desideria* in which he lashed out at the Lutheran State Church. He called for a total reform of the ministry with particular reference to the seminaries. He stressed genuine conversion, the new birth, a warm personal Christian experience, and the cultivation of Christian virtues. To summarize, the pietists promoted the serious study of the Bible, fostered vital piety, stressed the education of the young and ministers, and encouraged more active participation among the laity. This is the Evangelical United Brethren heritage. Otterbein was steeped in it and Albright put it into practice among his followers.

Although Ernest Stoeffler suggests that Otterbein "originally accepted this pietistic understanding of Christianity as a piece of intellectual equipment only," there can be little doubt that at some point the pietistic emphases (polished and softened by the Herborn School's emphasis on the *Heidelberg Catechism*) became Otterbein's personal experience, his badge of cause, initiating his own attempts at Christian unity within the context of fellowship and brotherly love.[1]

Watch carefully as the following events unfold.

Wir sind Brüder. The bloody barriers between the Mennonites and the churchly Protestants, such as the German Reformed, had been erected for many years with little sign of a breach. Imagine the significance of a meeting between Otterbein (a German Reformed) and Martin Boehm (a Mennonite) when Otterbein embraced Boehm in front of the *grosse versammlung* (great meeting) with the well-known words: *"Wir sind Brüder!"*

Boehm had called a great meeting (probably on Pentecost Sunday, 1767) in Isaac Long's barn near York where Otterbein was pastoring. Great meetings (a forerunner of the nineteenth century camp meetings) had been taking place in rural areas in the middle colonies since 1724. An announcement was made and people from the surrounding areas would gather, sometimes for several days, to hear great preaching and to fellowship among themselves. Otterbein attended this particular meeting not as a preacher but as one simply seeking fellowship with other German Christians. As Boehm began to preach, the stage was set.

78

Otterbein listened intently as Boehm bore witness to the gospel with a warm evangelical message that must have reminded Otterbein of his own "assurance experience" dating from 1754. With the invitation and benediction completed, Otterbein went forward to embrace Boehm with the words "We are brethren!"

Thus a friendship began which was ultimately the beginning of the United Brethren, at first a simple union of reborn German ministers and traveling preachers (both clergy and lay) committed to evangelism and renewal. They were encouraged to remain within their own churches (which included, among others, Reformed, Mennonite, Amish, and Moravian) while maintaining a further connection with a united fellowship in Christ. This fellowship instituted a new form of worship and evangelism primarily geared to the great meeting. Their goal was a united society among all German-American Christians. Their strong contention was that the primary focus of the gospel should not be upon faith as a system of dogma to be debated or defended among themselves, but an emphasis upon faith as a living experience of fellowship with God and each other. Equally important, the emphasis was on the people's freedom to respond once the gospel had been proclaimed. Their preaching, therefore, needed to be directed toward decision. The proclamation was clear—God's grace is at work. Receive Christ by faith and be reborn into fellowship with him and those around you. Finally, the preaching of the gospel must not be hindered by a particular polity or organizational structure as ends in themselves. Pride in denominational or traditional methods of operation was always secondary to the primary motive of promoting geniune piety. Whatever increased genuine piety was good; whatever decreased genuine piety was bad.

Following the establishment of this united fellowship, Otterbein quickly assumed leadership, although without formal election. Henry Spayth writes: "All eyes had been directed to him [Otterbein] to lead in counsel; the preachers, not one excepted, paid this *deference* to him; the care of all the Churches had been resting upon him, and such was the love of obedience to him, that if he said to one go, he went; if to another, come, he came." [2] Semiannual meetings (frequently in connection with the great meetings) were held by these ministers and traveling preachers at least from 1774 on, with somewhat of a lull during the war years due to the difficulty in travel. What took place at these early meetings is not fully known. It is suggested that some commissioning of lay participants to serve as evangelists took place. Remember, it was one of these lay evangelists who prayed with Albright at the time of his conversion.

79

After 1789 the meetings or conferences of this united fellowship became more and more formal. Yet it was 1800 before the United Brethren in Christ took its name and began looking toward official status.

September 25, 1800. Thus far we have observed Otterbein reaching out in brotherhood to any, regardless of religious affiliation, who would share in his vision for an evangelical proclamation of the gospel to the German-speaking people of America. This unity revealed itself in several of his attitudes. The "love feasts," for example, held at the close of the great meetings, were open to everyone and all left in true unity of spirit. This unity also revealed itself in his attitude toward the sacraments. In *The Church Book of 1785* (written for the Baltimore congregation and a forerunner to the first United Brethren *Discipline,* 1815) Rule 7 reads in part: "It becomes our duty, according to the Gospel, to commune with and admit to the Lord's table, professors, to whatever order or sort of the Christian church they belong." [3] Otterbein's only real concern was that he not form an additional sect. In light of this concern, the conference in 1800 is most interesting. At that conference both Otterbein and Boehm were apparently (although there is no mention of it in the minutes) chosen as superintendents. Let's look a bit closer.

On September 25, 1800, fourteen German ministers met in the home of Peter Kemp near Frederick, Maryland. The introductory historical summary to the 1815 United Brethren *Discipline* states that those at the 1800 conference elected William Otterbein and Martin Boehm as "superintendents or bishops." [4] According to the minutes for that meeting, the primary agenda was to establish a regular conference for these *unparteiisch* ("unsectarian") ministers. Although they had no intention of beginning a new sect or denomination, their "unsectarian" spirit merely disguised the inevitable. Another item not recorded in the minutes but mentioned by Henry Boehm (Martin's youngest son) in his *Reminiscences* was that "Father Otterbein made a move to get the Methodist *Discipline* translated. They all agreed to it. Praise the Lord. It appeared to me as if the Lord was pleased with it." [5] Admittedly the term *church* was not used until 1814, but some kind of an organization was clearly in the making. The United Brethren in Christ was well on its way in moving from fellowship, to society, to association, to church.

Although there was no official membership at first, there were those who were "authorized to perform all services of God's house." By 1813 several had been granted licenses to preach and formally ordained.

In line with Otterbein's passion for unity, the tone of the conferences following 1800 was warm and cordial. In addition to the stated agenda, each member reported on the year's activities including a word regarding his or her own present level of spirituality. Each was exhorted to preach earnest, vital, but not lengthy sermons. Each was expected to participate in the great meetings. A day or two of prayer and fasting was set aside each year for the entire "church." Appointments of ministers were made according to location and ministerial office. A preacher was appointed to each circuit and a superintendent was appointed to each district. Thus the movement prepared to announce its full identity. All that was needed was the opportunity. The death of Otterbein provided that opportunity and the United Brethren in Christ became the Church of the United Brethren in Christ soon afterward.

November 3, 1803. Little mention in this chapter has been made of Jacob Albright. Although Albright was American, born of Lutheran parents, he too became infected with the pietism of the more moderate Herborn School. There are several possible sources. The most obvious is Otterbein. Their contacts deeply impressed Albright. Although Albright held more closely defined views, the theology of his followers was basically pietistic with a similar emphasis on non-sectarian unity in Christ. He was constantly warning the Lutherans, Reformed, Dunkers, and Mennonites, not to trust their salvation to their churches' traditions, forms, and ceremonies. A change of heart brought about by the new birth, brought about by conversion, brought about by faith in Christ, was the only experience sufficient for salvation.

Like Otterbein, Albright formed classes. By 1803 there were five in all located in southeastern Pennsylvania. On November 3, 1803, Albright called a conference of class leaders to meet in the home of Samuel Lieisser in Berks County. George Miller (a new convert eventually to become an effective evangelist and a major Christian writer), was secretary.[6] He writes: "Forty, most of them blessed [converted] souls" were in attendance. Three main items stand out on the agenda. First, they established themselves as a new ecclesiastical organization. Second, they declared the scriptures to rule supreme with regard to doctrine and moral teaching. Third, they ordained Jacob Albright on November 5. This is the entry pertaining to that action: "In this year [1803] it was resolved that this association should establish a church substance and elected Jacob Albright as elder preacher. He was ordained and given the right to govern all meetings. . . . They gave him a certificate [which confirmed this action]."[7]

Thus the Evangelical Association (like the United Brethren before it) came to life. Although we cannot know for certain whether those

81

involved viewed this move as the creation of another denomination, subsequent interpretations made that a likely possibility. Albright, as the first "full" preacher, was its recognized leader. From this point on he was the one who was responsible for all appointments until the time of his death five years later.

The polity for the Evangelical Association was basically Methodist, while the theology was pietistic. Furthermore, their vision soon became worldwide. In the next fifty years, missions were established around the world. The work in Germany was especially productive. It made a deep impact upon the people there. I like the words of Steve O'Malley regarding Jacob Albright: "Such was the fruit of an obscure Pennsylvania farmer who became spiritually burdened for his neighbors and had a vision for God's work among his people." Albright, therefore, is not the end of the story. His followers were many and their influence significant. Let me illustrate with just a few cameos.

The Evangelical Association grew rapidly in the next few years. The preachers/evangelists who assisted Albright in traveling and establishing new circuits were mostly lay. I will mention just three. We have already made reference to George Miller (1774-1816). In spite of various illnesses which eventually took his life at forty-two, Miller was another tireless evangelist. In spite of all opposition, he persisted in his own faithful proclamation of the gospel. Many were critical of the "Albright people." Simply to be associated with them was cause enough for persecution. Nonetheless, Miller quickly distinguished himself as a great preacher. In fact, it was thought that he would assume leadership after Albright's death but a severe heart attack limited him to his own community where he continued to preach locally but spent most of his time writing.

Following Miller, other early leaders (such as Martin Dreisbach and John Walter) were either aged or also in ill health. Of the most effective assistants to Albright, only John Dreisbach (Albright's appointed assistant to Miller) was left to carry on. John Dreisbach (1789-1871) was the son of Martin Dreisbach, a deeply religious man and early supporter of Albright. John made a lasting mark upon the Evangelical Association. He directed the young church through years of growth and expansion. Like most of the Evangelical Association evangelists, Dreisbach experienced hardships in his extensive travels. Since his own health broke in 1821 (although he lived on for fifty years), his primary contribution from that time on was promoting the publication of religious materials. More will be said about this aspect of the Evangelical Association contribution in the next chapter.

Before moving on, however, there is an interesting story concerning Asbury and Dreisbach. Asbury attempted to persuade Dreisbach to leave the Evangelical Association and join the Methodists. Asbury promised that he would be assigned to a Methodist preacher for a year and that this preacher would assist him in improving his English. He would also, by joining the Methodists, guard against self-exaltation. Furthermore, Asbury added, the future of the German-speaking churches was limited in America and his association with the Methodists would increase his opportunities for ministry in the future. Dreisbach, however, thought that this move would be unfair to the Evangelical Association and self-serving. He proposed another plan to include the Evangelical Association as a Methodist circuit among the German-speaking Americans, but Asbury turned it down.

John Seybert (1791-1860) is still another significant figure in the Evangelical Association. Steve O'Malley refers to him as a "veritable St. Francis of the American frontier." [8] That may be somewhat of an exaggeration but not much. When Seybert joined with the Evangelicals, they numbered about 400 members. When he accepted the call to preach, he was one of only 20 itinerant evangelists who ministered to about 2000 members. By the time of his death, his church had grown to 40,000 members and there were nearly 600 itinerant and local preachers. Seybert was unmistakably a great man. He was both a traveling evangelist and a humanitarian — a good combination. He was genuinely pious, evangelical, frugal, charitable, and totally committed to Christ and church.

In 1839 he was elected bishop, the first since Albright. As bishop he was genuinely pious, evangelical, frugal, charitable, and totally committed to Christ and church. He continued to travel and preach against frightful circumstances. The Evangelical Association took root and grew in his path. He was always warm and personable. He made friends easily without compromising the gospel. Raymond Albright describes Seybert after a long hard day of traveling and preaching starting out late at night to visit a man who lived high on a mountainside. The next morning he returned rejoicing for having experienced the great joy of leading someone to Jesus Christ. [9] The last entry in his *Journal* reads appropriately: "Eine seele gerettet" (one soul saved). Samuel Spreng gives us these interesting statistics:

In these forty years he traveled per horse, one hundred and seventy-five thousand miles, preached about nine thousand eight hundred and fifty times, made about forty-six thousand pastoral visits, held about eight thousand prayer and class meetings, besides visiting at least ten thousand sick and afflicted ones.[10]

In addition Bishop Seybert was a gifted administrator. His leadership as evangelist/bishop/pastor was vital to the Evangelical Association through its more formative years. Again, Albright and many of his outstanding followers make us as United Methodists proud.

Schism. As fate would sometimes have it, both the United Brethren and the Evangelical Association, in spite of their passion for unity, to some degree, lost their primary vision and underwent wrenching internal divisions in the latter part of the nineteenth century. Briefly, let's look at them one at a time.

The Evangelical Association experienced growing tension for the thirty years prior to the 1887 general conference. Behney and Eller summarize the differences:

(1) Geographical sectionalism; (2) the use of the English language vs. German; (3) growth of episcopal authority; (4) rivalries for the office of bishop with attendant personal and party divisions; (5) the tendency toward democracy among members of longer American heritage vs. the tendency toward centralized authority of those of later immigration; and (6) disputes over such matters as appointment of representatives of the denomination to interdenominational activities.[11]

Many of the issues here seem petty and the debates inconsequential, but the pressure continued to build. Various church trials in effect canceled each other out. George Bernard Shaw's words: "Leave Christians alone, they'll kill each other" somehow seems appropriate. By 1891 the Evangelical Association had split into the Evangelical Association and the United Evangelical Church and remained so until reunion (alas, a happy ending) created the Evangelical Church in 1922.

During the same period there was also a schism within the United Brethren. With the United Brethren, however, there was no happy ending. The division there remains until this day. The issues focused in three areas: (1) lay delegates to general conference; (2) a reconstruction of the confession of faith (probably needed but difficult to manage); and (3) membership in secret societies (such as the Free Masons). A new constitution was proposed at the general conference for 1889 in York, Pennsylvania. It was adopted 110 to 20. Unfortunately the minority vote felt compromised and withdrew to form a new United Brethren in Christ (old constitution).

Union, 1946. On November 16, 1946, the Evangelical Church and the Church of the United Brethren in Christ united to become the Evangelical United Brethren. Before we lose our focus in too much historical data, allow me to get back to the impact of all this upon the evangelists. Where the evangelists were concerned, the issue was still the same. What was the role within a new body? Many changes had taken place since the early years of Otterbein and Albright. Were traveling preachers/evangelists still relevant in postwar 1946? Had the Evangelical United Brethren outgrown its revival tactics? The great meetings were certainly a thing of the past and the classes were also, by and large, either nonexistent or perfunctory.

Some of the issues affecting union also affected the role of the evangelists. The United Brethren had more of a rural orientation and were more low church in worship (the Mennonite influence) and less structured in polity than the Evangelical Church. By this time their German identity had all but disappeared. They retained a high social conscience. Contrarily, the Evangelical Church had more of an urban setting and was more orderly in liturgical worship (the Lutheran influence) and more structured in polity and episcopal rule. It had retained its German identity and placed a great deal of emphasis upon later holiness theology.

For the evangelists this meant reevaluation. With 800,000 EUB's, the temptation was to "hold the fort." Let's not rock the new boat. Fortunately the new EUB Church quickly established a general commission on evangelism with the express purpose of a united effort to win 75,000 to Christian discipleship. At this point, the evangelists might well have said: "We can win them but what will we do with them?" The classes (although there had been varied attempts to revive them across the years) were mostly a thing of the past. How do we disciple new Christians so that they are strengthened in their faith and sustained in their walk with Jesus Christ? Obviously the evangelists are still asking this important question.

Relevance for today. Both of the movements that eventually became the Evangelical United Brethren were fired in evangelism and looked for a united front to attack the forces of evil as one body. Raymond Albright gives us an interesting summation:

> The cycle of history had brought religious interest to a low ebb at the close of the 18th century. When formalism chilled religious fervor

and when there was little if any connection between religious profession and life, it was time that someone should call men to repentance for their sins and offer a more adequate way for making religion a practical experience in living. Under similar conditions the Reformers arose to rejuvenate the Christian religion which was dying in the 15th and 16th centuries. In a somewhat similar way, on a somewhat smaller scale, we have seen that men like Asbury, Otterbein, Boehm, and Albright called the attention of their contemporaries to the true nature of religion, its very close and practical relation with all aspects of living, and in half a century 1,000's to a religious experience which was intellectually valid, richly colored with emotional appeal, and morally controlling." [12]

Can the work of an evangelist still unite our efforts so that we can storm the very gates of hell as one? Perhaps we need to cast down the stereotype and look to those who set such an example. Not that we need another sect or denomination. God forbid, although the cutting edge of any denomination will split if the body cannot receive or affirm or contain it. There are those today who are willing to preach the gospel as evangelists within United Methodism. Do we need them or even want them? Can we disciple their converts? You bet we can—if we think it is important enough.

Chapter 9: EUB Distinctives

The messenger will undoubtedly be the unflinching advocate of true Evangelical preaching—Christ and him crucified, repentance toward God, faith in our Lord Jesus Christ, and deep, practical piety. . . .

The Evangelical Messenger (anonymous)

We have seen the United Brethren and the Evangelical Association (the Evangelical Church after 1922) unite to become the Evangelical United Brethren in 1946. It is time now to focus on some of the overall EUB distinctives in light of the history, role, and influence of the evangelist. Most of these distinctives have already surfaced in one form or another and all we need do now is to gather some of our thoughts to clarify our understanding.

We have already observed that evangelism was not closely tied to denominational identity among the United Brethren and Evangelical Association. Both groups displayed a willingness to surrender denominational identity in the interest of broader Christian unity in 1922 and 1946. This same spirit carried through to 1968 when United Methodism was formed. The term *United* is far more than an acknowledgment of our EUB legacy; it speaks of a pervading spirit that looks beyond sectarian interest to the greater causes of reaching the world for Christ and his kingdom. Methodism demonstrated this same spirit in 1939.

Unity is not the only distinctive, however. Here we will list some others and then seek to identify those issues most relevant for our study of the evangelist.

The influence of pietism establishes at least two important themes. First, evangelism was linked necessarily to practical Christian living. This revealed itself in an emphasis upon sanctification which included a deep social witness. For example, as a part of their teaching on holiness, both the United Brethren and the Evangelical Association stood unanimously opposed to slavery, child labor, and the abuse of alcohol and tobacco. Both recognized the evils of warfare and emphasized our accountability to God for such hostility. The issue of serving with the armed forces, however, was still left to personal choice.

87

The second influence of pietism related to the strong fusion of practical evangelism and certain mystical themes (especially among the leaders of the Evangelical Association).

Another EUB distinctive related to the strong congregational base for ministry (especially among the United Brethren). Although a connectional church, evangelism for the EUB was far more of a local church commitment than a program of the general conference.

Strong family orientation was still another EUB distinctive. Both the United Brethren and the Evangelical Association spread in the homes of large German-speaking farm families who scattered from early beginnings in Pennsylvania and Maryland across the Midwest in the nineteenth century. This family "home" flavor was important within the "EUB brotherhood" (a favorite term) as a whole.

The related themes of publishing Christian materials and education were also EUB distinctives. The Evangelical Association produced great indigenous hymn writers (John Walter and John Dreisbach) and devotional writers (George Miller and P. Hackenberg). The publishing houses within both movements were well known. Works from theological treatises to evangelistic tracts were widely distributed. There was also an increasing emphasis upon education. From church schools to seminaries the EUB passion was to sharpen every gift, whether spiritual or intellectual, for the cause of Christ.

From these distinctives let us look a bit closer at those areas most relevant for the evangelist. Since the previous chapter dealt with the issue of unity, here we will begin with the link between evangelism and practical Christian living.

Practical or living evangelism. Although our former EUB membership within United Methodism would be the first to admit that none of these distinctives is necessarily unique to the EUB heritage alone, there is an emphasis here (especially when combined with Methodism) that must not be forgotten.

In summarizing the legacy of the Otterbeins, Steve O'Malley, in his book *Pilgrimage of Faith*, makes an interesting observation:

Unlike later 19th-century revivalism, whose crusades tended to become the planned achievement of professional evangelists, this spirit was at heart truly evangelical—that is, it came as the surprising, unannounced visitation of God to men of faith and humility. It came with such power that its effects outlived the men who were its instruments. But this spirit of evangelicalism is not what is unique about the Otterbeins' message. . . . What *was* distinctive in their message was that fusion of German and Dutch Pietism, with its practical, "experimental" point of view, with the rich, evangelical themes of German Reformed theology, as embodied in the *Heidelberg Catechism*. This fusion of the "experiential" or the "experimental" with the sublime and the transcendent helped distinguish the Otterbeins from that later stream of American revivalism which sundered feeling from thought and will from intellect.[1]

In the contemporary idiom, the EUBs laid great emphasis upon "walking the talk." Christianity needed to manifest itself in everyday life. It needed to be practical. The Christian life was far more than right doctrine, or believing right things. It was a relationship built out of a commitment to God. The goal of Christianity was to bring every thought, every action under the lordship of Christ. Christianity made a difference in every area of life. All things relate to God or they relate to nothing. God is intimately transcendent. This evangelical, personal, "pietistic" relationship with God was also practical, social, and uncompromisingly insistent about service to others.

As the EUBs matured, the Christian response to poverty and social injustices involved far more than the giving of alms and the offering of prayers. Again, John Seybert sets the precedent. Raymond Albright writes that he "gave not only himself but all his means to the work of the church. He gave thousands of books to the poor and sold even greater numbers throughout the West. Bishop Seybert understood the value of religious literature. He loaned thousands of dollars to help those in stress. Once he purchased a widow's home at a sheriff sale and deeded it back to her and on another occasion purchased a weaver's loom from a sheriff who was taking it to be sold for the weaver's debts." [2] Personal morality extended to the deep-seated conviction that every man, woman, and child under God is precious and deserving of justice. God's redemption is individual and social. If humans can mess up society, by God's grace, they can clean up society. Remember, the United Brethren and Evangelical Association were predominantly a rural people in the nineteenth century. As industrialization and urbanization affected more and more of their constituents, personal piety became more and more of a public affair. Both the United Brethren and the Evangelical Association made decisive pronouncements concerning equal rights, the family, child labor, poverty, alcohol, the protection of workers, unions, the minimum wage, and more.[3]

In 1919 the bishops of the Evangelical Association in their quadrennial message stated: "Let us meet the industrial challenge from a sane and distinctively Christian standpoint, arraying ourselves against seven days' work and an unreasonable number of hours each day, for the better protection of working men against accidents, for sanitary conditions in factories and for moral restraints in places where workers of both sexes are employed." [4]

Mystical themes. We have already mentioned the EUB early understanding of an identification with Christ in suffering. There were other mystical themes as well. Albright, Miller, and Seybert were all deeply mystical in their approach to God. This experience described by Albright is typical:

> Naturally I had no talents to speak in public, and I frankly confess that I was less qualified in this respect than any other who might have undertaken it; but when I felt myself carried away by the Spirit of God, when prayer brought my soul nearer to my Redeemer, when I was animated with a hatred against sin, when the righteousness of a scrutinizing Judge appeared before me, and I at the same time realized his overwhelming love toward his fallen creatures, I was seized upon by an influence which loosened my tongue, and God's grace wrought through me the conversion of fallen and unconverted professors of religion, and the edification of true believers. [5]

As for George Miller, some skeptics might attribute many of his experiences to bouts with a permanently damaged heart (probably a result of rheumatic fever suffered as a child), but one still has to account for the many experiences of John Seybert. We have already met Seybert on several occasions. Although not known for his preaching, his life manifested the mind of Christ in many, many ways. Again, Raymond Albright states that he "was fundamentally of a deeply mystical nature." [6] We are not surprised that the most prominent books in his voluminous library were pietistic and mystical works.

Local church evangelism. We noted in the last chapter that the EUB upon union in 1946 developed a church-wide program for evangelism. What we left unsaid was that the EUB emphasis laid the greatest burden for evangelism upon the local church.

Otterbein no doubt set the precedent. As a pastor/evangelist he saw the importance of attaching new converts to classes which then became incredibly effective in their witness for Christ. As in early Methodism, many of those won to Christ were won within the small groups of predominantly lay men and women. It would be difficult to exaggerate the loss sustained by the church as a result of the decline of these small groups. This was the local church at work in evangelism at its very best. The local church "chattering" the gospel is a powerful witness for Jesus Christ.

Even today most people are won and then sustained one on one. The evangelist can minister most effectively by getting others to share their faith as opportunity arises.

Household evangelism. Related to local church evangelism is household evangelism. Again, we have noted that most of the work of the early evangelists in American Methodism as well as in the EUB connections took place in private homes. The "great meetings" provided the heat to bake the bread but the homes of Christians prepared the dough and shaped the loaves.

During his own ministry Jesus was constantly in the homes of people. Like Jesus, the early evangelists easily accepted hospitality. The neighbors were then gathered, the Word was preached, and God was glorified.

Literary evangelism. The EUB appreciation for the power of the printed word is well known by those with even a cursory knowledge of the movements that united in 1946. We have already mentioned George Miller who wrote and Bishop Seybert who, if he was not selling, was giving away thousands of religious books for the express purpose of evangelism.

There is no excuse for an evangelist preaching from a dusty corpus of sermons that rarely changes. Those who read are constantly renewing their minds. Fresh insights are flowing constantly. Those who do not read become stale and ineffective. Wesley's words are right on target. He writes in a letter in 1760:

What has exceedingly hurt you in time past, may be, and I fear to this day, is want of reading. I scarce ever knew a preacher read so little. And perhaps by neglecting it you have lost the taste for it. Hence your talent in preaching does not increase. It is just the same as it was seven years ago. It is lively, but not deep; there is little variety; there is no compass of thought. Reading only can supply this, with meditation and daily prayer. You wrong yourself greatly by omitting this. You can never be a deep preacher without it anymore than a thorough Christian. Oh begin! Fix some part of everyday for private exercises. You may acquire the taste which you have not; what is tedious at first will afterwards be pleasant. Whether you like it or no, read and pray daily. It is for your life; there is no other

91

way: else you will be a trifler all your days and a pretty superficial preacher.[7]

The United Brethren and the Evangelical Association heeded Wesley's admonition. Since books in German were not always readily available, publishing houses were established almost immediately to circulate German-translated Christian classics. The intent was obvious. Read this introductory remark in the early devotional book by P. Hackenberg entitled *A Short Review of the Most Important Teachings of the Christian Religion*: "Out of his [Hackenberg's] and others' writings, [he] tried to lead readers into the good old way. Jesus is the way, the only way to the Father; the living way to holiness, bliss and to heaven"[8]

The Evangelical Association also published one of the earliest Christian newspapers (*Der Christliche Botschafter*) along with several periodicals. *Der Christliche Botschafter* had 25,000 subscribers by the end of the nineteenth century. Then with the ever-widening sanction of the use of the English language, the *Evangelical Messenger* appeared in 1848. Here are a few of the early testimonials:

> *The Messenger* will undoubtedly be the unflinching advocate of true Evangelical preaching—Christ and him crucified, repentance toward God, faith in our Lord Jesus Christ, and deep, practical piety. . . . We expect the *Messenger* will at proper times and in proper places oppose the corruptions of the age in which we live. . . . We trust that no organization, deleterious to the true interest of the Gospel, will receive any sanction from this periodical; but that the unfruitful works of darkness will be reproved, and the light of the Gospel of Jesus Christ allowed to shine in every corner of the land, and to every department of the society, as a guide to the young, an instructor of the ignorant, and a help to the benighted and wayward traveler.[9]

The training of evangelists. Related to publications is education. More and more the United Brethren and the Evangelical Association emphasized the training of their constituents from church school through college, and, for those called, through seminary. The objective of the latter was to train men and women for Christian service. The minister of the gospel needed no less training for his or her important work than other professionals. The evangelist could best prepare by securing the proper tools for rightly dividing the word of truth (2 Tim.

2:15). As we have already noted, the evangelist must not only preach, but insure opportunity for growth and nurture. More and more, the evangelist is a teacher and discipler as well as preacher.

Relevance for today. Each of these distinctives draws a more inclusive portrait of the evangelist. Today the gifted preacher must have additional skills as well.

The evangelist today had best be practical in a society where non-practicality is carted off as hypocritical and irrelevant. If the evangelist does not live the talk, then something about his or her ministry will not ring true. Elmer Gantry is dead.

Furthermore, the gospel must be relevant to everyday life. My own association with Oral Roberts has proven time and again that people respond to a God who cares about practical needs. Similarly, people want to experience this God in a personal way. The mystical experiences of assurance and faith are still drawing crowds the world over.

A congregational base for evangelism reiterates the importance of the local church. Evangelists are still most effective in a local church setting where follow-up is assured. Also, lay evangelism, especially within the local fellowship, must not be overlooked.

Similarly, in-home evangelism is still a viable method of reaching the lost for Christ. Recently, more, rather than less, emphasis has been placed upon small groups ranging from kaffeeklatsches to prayer and Bible studies as a means of providing a viable setting for relational evangelism.

Literary evangelism has obviously graduated from passing out tracts on street corners to the promotion of attractive books, magazines, and newspapers designed to confront even casual readers with the claims of the gospel upon their lives.

Education is still a must. Billy Graham has been quoted as saying that if he were certain that Jesus Christ would not return for four years, he would spend three of those years in seminary. Although none of us knows for certain when Christ will return, for many of us seminary is worth the risk.

The EUB legacy is a great one. Our *United* Methodist roots are varied and deep. Again, we can all be proud.

Part IV
The Contemporary Scene

Chapter 10: The E. Stanley Jones Model

Jesus is Lord!

Fortunately, the role and influence of the evangelist in United Methodism is not just history. There have been and are great evangelists in our own time. Their importance has not diminished. Part IV is an honest attempt to make that point clear and unmistakable.

When deciding on a model for this last part, I sought help. I asked several who had distinguished themselves as evangelists in their own right to give an opinion as to who on the contemporary scene best epitomizes the evangelist within United Methodism. The name E. Stanley Jones quickly rose to the top. Quite frankly he was my choice as well. There is a reason for that. I heard him teach and preach. I have read his books. He was a remarkable man and a great evangelist. True, he was more than an evangelist in the narrower sense of that term, but that (in part) is the intent of this book—to broaden our vision for the work of an evangelist. Stanley Jones serves our purpose well. He not only proclaimed the gospel faithfully, he was constantly setting new trends, many of which will carry us into the twenty-first century.

Introduction. Eli Stanley Jones (or Brother Stanley as he preferred to be called) was born in Maryland in 1884. Who can really capture his indomitable spirit? All we can do is jot down a few thoughts like an occasional snapshot in a photo album. Fortunately, he has told his own story in several books. Perhaps the best source for understanding the mind and spirit of Stanley Jones is his spiritual autobiography entitled *A Song of Ascents.* Read it along with some of his twenty-eight other books. They may well change your life.

Brother Stanley was converted in his teens. After high school he struggled (working in a law library and then collecting and writing industrial insurance in a poor section of Baltimore) to raise enough money to enter and then finish Asbury College. While at Asbury, he tells us that God called him to be a missionary/evangelist. Following graduation he had several options. He had been invited to stay on and teach at Asbury. He had also been encouraged to remain in America as a traveling evangelist. Then the Methodist Mission Board offered to send him to India. He chose India.

India took all or part of Brother Stanley's time for the next sixty years or more. His preaching, traveling, and writing consumed him. In 1907 he was appointed to Lal Bogh, the English-speaking church in Lucknow. During his four years there, along with his responsibilities to the local congregation, he worked hard on languages and ministered to the outcasts from the Indian society. He also developed a deep understanding of the Indian culture and religions. Eventually, he felt drawn to the intellectuals of India. He sought to interpret Christianity, not as a Western import, but as the fulfillment of everyone's longing. He often quoted the well-known lines from Augustine: "We are made for God, and we are restless till we rest in Him."

In 1928 Stanley Jones was elected Bishop but quickly resigned to carry on his work as a missionary/evangelist. As a thorough-going evangelist, Brother Stanley proclaimed the gospel of Jesus Christ to thousands of people. Yet his preaching had tremendous balance. He can also be seen taking strong stands for social justice in general, and peace, racial equality, and Christian unity in particular. In 1930 he founded the Christian Ashram movement at Sal Tal. The Ashram is a retreat fashioned after a Hindu model but with Jesus Christ as the "guru." Many of us remember Brother Stanley with three fingers thrust into the air as a sign of the simplest of all the Christian creeds — *Jesus is Lord.* Those three words capture his message, describe the secret to his character, the key to his style, and the strength of his motivation.

Message. E. Stanley Jones was a missionary but he was foremost an evangelist. The evangelistic thrust of his message was the heart of his greatness. His life was committed to reaching the world for Jesus Christ. Before he was twenty, he had already led many (including his 82-year-old grandmother) to Christian conversion.

Conversion for Brother Stanley was key. To speak of Jesus Christ forces a personal decision. Arguments over creation or the gifts of the Spirit do not lead to conversion. Christ alone forces the ultimate decision. Listen as Brother Stanley speaks of his own conversion:

It took an emotional upheaval to carry me across from a self-preoccupied life to a Christ-preoccupied life. The center of being was changed from self to Savior. I didn't try by an act of will to give up my sins — they were gone. I looked into his face and was forever spoiled for anything that was unlike him. The whole me was converted. There was nothing the same except my name. It was the birthday of my soul. Life began there. Note I say "began"—the whole of my life has been an unfolding of what was infolded in that moment.[1]

Stanley Jones' whole approach was Christocentric. For him, Christianity was Christ. In the *Christ of the Indian Road* he writes:

I was holding a very long line before the non-Christian world, a line that stretched from Genesis to Revelation, on to the Christian church and to Western civilization. Like many others I was bobbing up and down the line fighting behind Moses and David and Jesus and Paul and Western civilization, and the Western church built up around Christ. I was sweating, trying to hold such a long line. The non-Christian almost invariably pitched the battle at the Old Testament or at Western civilization or the Christian church. I felt the heart of the matter was being left out—Christ. So I decided to shorten my line and take my stand at Jesus Christ and refuse to know anything before that non-Christian world save Jesus Christ and him crucified. I would bring everything to him. My task was simplified.[2]

The absolute uniqueness of Christ was not in degree but kind. The Word did not become word, it became flesh. Christianity was person, not concept. Christ did not bring good news, he was good news. In the words of Origen, Christ was "kingdom in person."

The incarnation held sheer fascination for Stanley Jones. He spoke and wrote about it in profound but simple terms. These next words could be around for a hundred years:

When the Scripture says that Jesus is the Word, I see the necessity of the Word. Words are the expression of the hidden thought, and without a word you cannot understand the thought. Yet the word and the thought are one. When you take hold of the word you take hold of the thought. But the thought is greater than the word, for all expression of the thought limits it. God, the eternal Spirit, is the hidden thought. He reveals himself in the Word, Jesus. Since the Thought and the Word are one, Jesus could say, "I and the Father are one." When you take hold of Jesus, you take hold of God. Jesus is not a third something between me and God—he is God available. When you take hold of Jesus, you take hold of the very self of God. He is a mediator only in the sense that he mediates God to you. But he also said, "The Father is greater than I." If he and the Father are "one," how is it that the Father is greater? But that is true of the thought and the word. The thought and the word are one, and yet the unexpressed thought is greater than the expressed word. For all expression means limitation. You have to search for words to express the thought. So the unexpressed God—the Father—is greater than the expressed Word—the Son. And yet they are "one."[3]

Brother Stanley's message was deep for the deep, yet simple enough for the unsophisticated. The Bible held a special place in all of his preaching and teaching. He would pore over it for hours in a rat-infested shed in some remote part of India. He stated unashamedly: "While I am not a fundamentalist or a modernist, only a Christian-in-the-making, I do love this book, for these words take me beyond the words to the Word."[4] The question of authority always *began* in the Bible as objective reality which then became the subjective reality of experience which was then corrected and corroborated by the collective witness of the church.

The integrity of Christianity for Brother Stanley always focused in Jesus Christ. Christ became his refuge. When under attack he spoke only of Jesus. Jesus Christ was the divine "Yes" to all of the world's no's. Again, he writes: "Now in the midst of this world chorus of No, at last—at long last—'the divine "yes" has sounded.' And Jesus is that Yes. This is a new, a startling note in a world whose pessimism has reduced the world's music to a minor key. There are no 'Hallelujah Choruses' in ancient or modern non-Christianity."[5]

We have already mentioned that Stanley Jones was a trend setter. Let me give you an example. Over fifty years ago he wrote a book on Pentecost entitled *The Christ of Every Road*. Long before the many books which have been written on the Holy Spirit (especially in the last ten to fifteen years) Brother Stanley was emphasizing the power of the Holy Spirit available to all in Jesus Christ. Admittedly, he was weary of arguments over tongues and other good gifts of the Spirit. He simply believed that the call of the evangelist was to make Christians out of non-Christians, not Pentecostals out of Protestants and Catholics. For many years Brother Stanley presented the Holy Spirit as a present reality who, as the fullness of God himself, brought power to life and witness. Again, he gives us a striking personal testimony. After accepting God's offer of the Holy Spirit, he writes:

I arose from my knees, with no evidence, save his word. I walked out on the naked promise of that Word. His character was behind that Word. I could trust him with my all and I could trust him to give me his all. I walked around the room repeating my acceptance. The doubts began to close in on me. I did what Abraham did when the birds came to scatter his sacrifice—he shooed them away. I walked around the room pushing away with my hands the meancing doubts. When suddenly I was filled—filled with the Holy Spirit. Wave after wave of the Spirit seemed to be going through me as a cleansing fire. I could only walk the floor with the tears of joy flowing down my cheeks. I could do nothing but praise him—and did. I knew this was no passing emotion; the Holy Spirit had come to abide with me forever.[6]

The gift of the Holy Spirit for Brother Stanley brought purity and power. It brought purity for himself and for his own inner needs, and power to witness effectively to others.[7]

There was much about Brother Stanley that was refreshingly open and honest. He rarely failed to make good sense. He was never afraid to ask the obvious question. For example, he would ask: "What business are we in? What does Christ have to offer?" The answer? Simple—the fulfillment of everyone's dream—a relationship with a living God who loves them personally. Culturally, Brother Stanley was wise enough to avoid the obvious blunder but naive enough to keep his vision. Many of us know too much. We are too wise and too learned as to why something will not work or why something cannot be done. God forgive our little faith.

Stanley Jones' trend setting took another turn in 1930 with the establishment of the Christian Ashram movement. Built on the Hindu model of retreat, or time spent under the watchful eye of some noted teacher or guru, Christ himself became the guru for the Christian Ashram. Everything and everyone finds focus in Jesus. Brother Stanley's book *Victorious Living* describes the Ashram: "In our Ashram we bring together people of differing outlooks and temperaments and races and theological beliefs and we undertake to make a brotherhood out of these differences."[8]

This raises still another important aspect of Stanley Jones' message. Again, the focus was always Christ, but Christ spoke to many issues. Brother Stanley was socially, politically, and ecclesiastically astute. He longed for union among nations and people, but especially among Christians. He spoke of Federal union as the key. He envisioned it for countries (India and Pakistan). He envisioned it for people (abolishing

101

the abhorred caste system). He envisioned it for the church (Catholic, Protestant, Orthodox). More will be said about his concept of Federal union under the discussion of style, but for now the key is oneness in Jesus Christ. In *The Christ of the American Road* he writes: "For none of us has the Truth. The Truth is in Christ—the Truth. What we hold is truths about the Truth. We need, therefore, the other person's truth to add to our truths, so that our pooled truths may more closely approximate him who is *the* Truth."[9]

Brother Stanley also set trends in the areas of racial integration and women's rights. The Ashrams were free of caste and title in India (hence *Brother* Stanley). They were free of race and sex discrimination in America. Every Ashram is fully integrated. Women are prominent, even in India. In light of the Buddhist teaching that a woman must be reborn as a man if she is to attain salvation, this was a significant breakthrough. In America the most prominent roles of Ashram evangelist, Bible teacher, or Church in Action speaker frequently go to women like Anna Mow, Mary Webster, or Geraldine Conway.

In his *A Song of Ascents* Brother Stanley gives a summary of all his teaching. There are thirty conclusions. The primary focus is unmistakably Jesus Christ as the revelation of God as One who wants us to receive from him an abundant victorious Christian life through the power of the Holy Spirit.

Character. Stanley Jones was appalled by the inconsistency between "walk and talk" among many Christians. He reminds us that India went through three stages in her response to Christianity. It isn't true. It isn't new. It isn't *you.* He could speak convincingly to the first two responses. The third was not so easily obviated. Again, Christians will be heard with authority to the precise degree that they are willing to put their lives on the line. "Jesus is Lord" means that once we repent and believe, we seek his inspiration and power in all that we do. Brother Stanley sought to live his faith even in the most difficult times. He sought to follow Jesus outwardly and inwardly as well. Once again he bears personal witness:

> He had been with me, with me in the conscious mind in conversion. Now he was in me, in me in the subconscious. When he was with me in the conscious, it was conversion limited, for the subconscious was not redeemed; cowed and suppressed, but not redeemed. Now the subconscious was redeemed. These drives which reside in the subconscious—self, sex, and the herd—were cleansed; the self-urge cleansed from selfishness, the sex urge from sexuality, the herd urge

102

from being fastened on society was now refastened on the Kingdom of God, the ultimate society. With these drives redeemed it was conversion unlimited, nothing left out of its sway.[10]

Brother Stanley, like our previous models, taught that opposition/persecution can either break or solidify. He emphasized time and again that everything, good, bad, or indifferent can be used for God's glory. He illustrated with his own life. Our earlier description as an "indomitable spirit" was more than a catch phrase. He was joy and hope itself. He had sparkle. He was selfless in many ways. He gave from all of his spiritual and material resources, supporting students with prayer and money around the world. He was a wealthy man, for God supplied all of his needs. Yet he was wealthiest (materially speaking) in the "fewness of his wants." I am not surprised that he was fond of that last phrase.

Not to dodge the obvious issues, Brother Stanley dealt openly and honestly with basic morality. I heard him confess to sexual temptation at the age of eighty-eight. He addressed the topic of sex in such a manner as to portray it as a gift of God to be celebrated in marriage as a bond between husband and wife, but nowhere else.

Style. Two words already used at least twice give clue to Brother Stanley's style—*open* and *honest.* His preaching had more the character of witness than exhortation. This was his peculiar (for lack of a better word) genius. He was always at his best telling people what God had done for him. Why? Because God had done so much and he knew it. That was not an idle boast. It was the deepest humility. Brother Stanley liked to give credit where credit was due—not that he credited everything good to God as if he could not accept responsibility for his own actions. Stanley Jones simply knew his limitations. Depending upon God to give him a word or a piece of bread became a way of life.

Brother Stanley's style was to see people in the whole. He rarely saw Hindus or Muslims, Christians or non-Christians. He saw people in spiritual need—in need of a Savior.[11] That is the stuff that evangelism is made of. His style was warmhearted, person-to-person, not preacher-to-audience. He was rarely argumentative. He determined to "shorten his line" from verbal to vital, from inconclusive to conclusive, from mere proclamation to proclamation/presence, from static to dynamic, from perfection achieved to perfection in process, from disputation to witness, witness, witness.

The witness approach keeps us moving, growing as our relationship with God grows. The more he does for us the more we have to share. If nothing is happening, we soon have nothing to say that is vital and fresh. We quickly become stale and repetitive. Witness is present reality; it is present experience. Brother Stanley gives a beautiful description of this kind of reality:

There are two kinds of reality—objective reality and subjective reality, the reality of history and the reality of experience. Each of these kinds of reality can bring a high degree of certainty. For instance, objective reality, the reality of history, can be seen in the Battle of Waterloo. Waterloo can be proved by historical investigation to a high degree of certainty. It is beyond question. But not the highest degree of certainty. For it is objective reality, not subjective reality. I for one did not experience Waterloo, though I believe in it. But certain things have gone through the stream of my experience, and I know that I know and am sure that I am sure. "He who says experience says science." So subjective reality can be proved to a high degree of certainty. But not the highest degree. The highest degree of certainty would come where the two kinds of reality—the objective and the subjective—would come together, dovetail, speak the same thing, and thus corroborate each other.[12]

Along this same line, Brother Stanley believed in growth toward Christian maturity. As a young Christian his book entitled *Christian Maturity* gave me new hope when things had seemingly leveled off in my spiritual walk. Stanley Jones also looked for new ways of describing age-old truths—a new vocabulary. For this reason, most of his books have staying power. I have just reread much of *Christian Maturity*, written in 1957. It is just as relevant today as then.

At this point more must be said about two things of utmost importance to Brother Stanley—the Ashram and his vision for a worldwide Federal union among Christians.

The Ashram movement represented a great deal of what was Stanley Jones at his core. It began with an interest in the classes. He describes the process himself. If you will stay with this next quotation, there is probably something in it for you:

I mentioned above the class meeting. This class meeting, where we told our successes and failures, our joys and our problems, became for me the germ of an idea which has blossomed into a world movement—the Christian Ashram movement. Everyone needs a close-knit fellowship to which he is responsible and which is responsible for him. I found it in the class meetings. And found it when I needed it most. I always looked forward with joy to tell of the victories of the week. For there were victories, almost continuous victories. For months after conversion I was running under cloudless skies. And then suddenly I tripped, almost fell, pulled back this side of the sin, but was shaken and humiliated that I could come that close to sin. I thought I was emancipated and found I wasn't. I went to the class meeting—I'm grateful that I didn't stay away—went, but my music had gone. I had hung my harp on a weeping willow tree. As the others spoke of their joys and victories of the week, I sat there with the tears rolling down my cheeks. I was heartbroken. After the others had spoken, John Zink, the class leader, said: "Now, Stanley, tell us what is the matter." I told them I couldn't, but would they please pray for me? Like one man they fell to their knees, and they lifted me back to the bosom of God by faith and love. When we got up from our knees, I was reconciled to my heavenly Father, to the group, and to myself. I was reconciled. The universe opened its arms and took me in again. The estrangement was gone. I took my harp from the willow tree and began to sing again—the Song of Moses and the Lamb, especially the Lamb. The cross was my refuge and my release.[13]

The Ashram expanded on the class meetings so that most Ashrams now run for a week in a retreat setting where the focus for the plenary sessions is on evangelistic preaching, Bible study, and an exchange of ideas for the church in action. There is much time for silence and prayer. There is much time for fellowship. The week begins with a session called the "open heart." Here people describe their needs. The week concludes with a session called the "overflowing heart." Here people describe how these (and other) needs have been met—a witness. Thousands of people have been won to Christ through these Ashrams. Why? Because the overall theme is summarized by three words. You guessed it—Jesus is Lord.

We have also mentioned Brother Stanley's passion for a Federal union. Let him describe it for the church:

There would be one Church in America: the Church of Jesus Christ in America. . . .That church would be an organic union; both merger and federal union want organic union—one with a monolithic structure and the other with a federal structure. The United States of America is an organic union: it can act as a single organism, but it has a federal structure. So federal union is not a council—it is union. The union is sovereign.

But under the Church of Jesus Christ in America there would be branches, no longer churches, separate and sovereign, but branches of the one church. . . . Within those branches there could be local self-government, states' rights, provincial autonomy. . . .

Over these branches there would be a General Assembly of the Church of Jesus Christ in America made up of representatives from all the branches. The General Assembly would be the sovereign body. It would have to do with everything that concerned the church as a whole: a strategy and program for evangelism, for missions, for education at home and abroad, and all of the subjects assigned to it by a constitutional convention. The rest of the subjects would remain in the branches. Under the General Assembly there would be a state assembly, a county assembly, a city assembly, a town assembly of the Church of Jesus Christ in America. In the county, city, and town assemblies we could deal with the questions of overlapping and competition on the local level.[14]

This description goes on for several pages but that gives you a bit of the flavor. Brother Stanley remarks of his vision: "This is what I saw. Take it, criticize it, pull it to pieces and find its weaknesses if it has them, and its strengths if it has them, and offer a better substitute—if there is one."[15]

Motivation. When describing his early days in India, Brother Stanley makes this observation:

All I knew was evangelism—people needed to be converted, to be changed. So I proceeded to act on that faith. My first sermon was on the text "Thou shalt call his name Jesus: for he shall save his people from their sins" (Matt. 1:21). A Savior, not *in* their sins, but from their sins. In the morning services I would talk on the deeper life, the Holy Spirit, cleansing, for the regulars, the "saints" were present. At night the masses would come. They packed the church, and my theme was conversion in its varying phases. I gave an altar call at each night's service, and for four years every Sunday we had conversions, except for two Sundays; and on those two Sundays it was too hot for anybody to decide anything.[16]

Isn't it clear by now that the consistent motivation for any evangelist worth his or her salt is the care for souls? Are the issues really important, life and death, heaven and hell, light and darkness, freedom and bondage, love and hate? Any Christian who thinks that Jesus Christ makes that kind of a difference will not rest until the whole world knows that Jesus is Lord.

Relevance for today. Although Stanley Jones has been dead for over a decade (he died in 1973), most of his ideas and approaches are fresh as today. He is truly a contemporary.

Much of that which is relevant for today in E. Stanley Jones is by now wonderfully repetitive from previous chapters. The gospel proves that old saying: The more things change the more they are the same. Yet Stanley Jones has a way of reiterating the essentials and bringing them up-to-date as if to remind us of forgotten dreams. Let me illustrate.

Christianity and the proclamation of the evangelist must constantly renew its focus in Jesus Christ. It is that simple. Throughout our modeling chapters the emphasis has been on Jesus Christ, yet Brother Stanley found his message and refuge (witness and experience) in Christ alone. While living in Chicago I opened my newspaper one morning to read the headlines: "Christ Called Answer to Man's Emptiness." The article underneath began with these words: "The way of Jesus should be—but often isn't—the way of Christianity; this is the conviction of a Christian who, at 80, acts like a young man still on the way up. 'The one thing we have to give is the person of Jesus Christ, rather than the organized system (the church) built up around Him in the West,' said [you guessed it] the Reverend E. Stanley Jones."[1]

Brother Stanley's emphasis on the Holy Spirit is vital for today. So much is being said today about the Holy Spirit that not to speak clearly is to speak too much by default. People will hear what they want to hear if they are not told plainly just what you mean. More will be said about this in our final chapter.

The Ashram movement is relevant for today. Furthermore, within Methodism alone, there are similar opportunities for renewal such as the Emmaus Walk, Lay Academies, Lay Witness Missions, New Life Missions, just to mention a few. The opportunities for the evangelists today either to tie into or to encourage as follow-up are all around us.

Ecumenism is not dead at the level above organization. Brother Stanley's dreams for Federal union might have been a bit naive, but he was no fool. If we Christians at some point do not proclaim (to use Otterbein's phrase) an "unsectarian" gospel that unites people across denominational lines, we may well be speaking only among ourselves in the not-too-distant future.

Let's close on a more positive note. The gospel, in the spirit of E.

Stanley Jones, is not "I've got it and you need it." It is "Jesus Christ has me and he will have you, too." Last week I read that the Unitarians are debating whether or not to drop the name *God* from their language altogether in favor of a purely humanistic terminology. Here is a statement from E. Stanley Jones written in the 1950s: "A man belonging to a group with a Unitarian emphasis came to me and said: 'Will you come to our convention and help us to find God? We are drifting into humanism.' Here was a group specializing on God and losing Him, and here was I, specializing on Jesus and finding Him."[18] Relevant? You bet your life it is.

Chapter 11:
The Evangelists Come of Age

Good preaching, like good theology, is balance without compromise.

Admittedly the heading for this chapter sounds like a bit of presumption. If I might anticipate your response (still more presumption) allow me to ask a few questions in order to clarify some of the pertinent issues. What do I mean by evangelists come of age? Have I not been telling you that this great church of ours was built largely on the strength of its evangelists? Were they not already of age? Did something go wrong? In our race to the contemporary scene, did we miss something important? Where are we now? I believe that these are fair questions. Let me address them under the following outline: the scene changes; evangelism gone sour; evangelism catches up; the evangelist comes of age; and the relevance for today.

The scene changes. In our move through history, the nineteenth century was something of a blur, That, in a sense, was unfair. The nineteenth century was a time of great evangelists. Although historians have spilled most of their ink on men like Finney and Moody, there were great EUB (see Part III) and Methodist evangelists as well. Let me illustrate.

Maggie Van Cott was the first woman licensed to preach in the Methodist Episcopal Church in the United States. During her first year of ministry (1869) she delivered 335 sermons, traveled 3,000 miles, and added 500 new members to the Methodist Church.[1] She advertised special meetings for mothers, old veterans, and children. She also established praise meetings, silent meetings, and love feasts. At the close of each of her revivals she organized prayer bands for new converts and church members in order to sustain the revival spirit. One-half of those converted in her meetings became members of Methodist churches, and three-fourths of those who joined became "good working Christians."[2]

Samuel Porter Jones and Ira Sankey were also well-known nineteenth century Methodist evangelists. Samuel Jones, a recovered alcoholic, was admitted to the North Georgia Conference of the Methodist Episcopal Church South in 1872. Beginning with five small churches scattered in four different counties, it soon became apparent that he was no ordinary preacher. As he was invited to preach in neighboring towns his fame grew. He was soon preaching across the land, frequently in tobacco or cotton warehouses or even in bush arbors. In several places special wooden tabernacles were built for him. He once held a revival in a renovated skating rink in Chicago that held 7,000. The total attendance for a five-week period was estimated at over a quarter million. The total attendance figures for most of his meetings were in the neighborhood of 150,000.

Ira Sankey was still another Methodist evangelist, well known for his hymn writing. Most would agree that as a song leader his close association with D. L. Moody contributed largely to Moody's success.

Yet, in spite of the fact that there were great evangelists in the nineteenth century, the new urban-industrial society presented a challenge that most could not answer. The theological scene was also changing. We have heard E. Stanley Jones use the word *modernist*. Let me attempt to explain it in capsule.

Modernism sprang out of the liberalism of the nineteenth century. Liberal theology incorporates the values of modern political and social movements into Christian systematic thinking. The ethical is emphasized over the doctrinal aspects of Christianity. Ultimately the greatest stress is upon human freedom and our ability to respond to God's will and our capacity to shape our own futures.

Even though liberalism predates modernism, the two are closely related. Although there are some positive aspects of modernism, the term has been used among evangelicals largely in a derogatory sense to characterize the variety of post-Kantian theologies that have become popular in Protestant churches during the twentieth century. These theologies have uniformly adopted the "higher critical" approach which challenges the uniqueness of revelation in general and questions the ability of the scriptures to provide humankind with an adequate knowledge of God. For example, they have, for the most part, abandoned the classic Christian doctrines of creation, the fall, and justification by faith in Jesus Christ. As in liberalism, modernists have attempted to reconstruct the Christian faith along purely ethical lines in accordance with the "modern findings" of science and history. The progress of the kingdom of God is understood in terms of social and political improvement. Even more damaging is that in New Testament

110

studies, modernism, in an attempt to accommodate the modern mind, has "de-supernaturalized" the historical Jesus.

Beginning with theologians such as Gotthold Lessing (1729-1781), the purely rational/historical mind of liberalism reached an impasse in its approach to God, called the "ugly ditch." Since faith alone approaches the throne of God—faith in the Son, faith in the Word—there was always that one last step beyond sight. Predictably, the issues soon became biblical. Schleiermacher (known as the father of liberalism) concluded that the scriptures could not be the basis for faith since faith was needed to read them.

Harnack and Herrmann personify liberalism. Harnack argued that dogma was the outgrowth of a Greek spirit in the soil of the gospel. He sought, through an insipid reductionism, to reduce the truth of the Bible to the simple eithical religion of Jesus which had been obscured (so he thought) by the encrustation of church dogma. The emphasis here was in doing, not believing. The issue of Christianity was in the teachings of Jesus, not in proclamation about him.

Herrmann's more subtle experientialism agrees with Harnack that Christianity is not dogma. According to Herrmann, biblical truth does not communicate salvation; salvation is an experience or communion with God. It is purely a personal matter. Dogma, Christ, Bible, simply confirm personal experience. Faith is not an assent to doctrine but receiving and using what God gives us when God comes inwardly near us.

Close behind the ethical emphasis of liberalism was Walter Rauschenbusch (known as the father of the social gospel). Liberalism/modernism turned to the social gospel as its badge of cause. Since Christianity was not believing, then it must be doing.

To summarize, the end result of modernism has been an emphasis upon (1) anthropology as the knowledge of God begins within the human intellect and works "upward"; (2) an ethical religion leaning toward works righteousness and social justice over and against the proclamation of the gospel as first of all faith in Jesus Christ as an atonement for sin; and (3) a reduced emphasis on the Bible as the Word of God and on Christ as the unique Son of God. In effect, Christianity during the first four decades of this century was split in two—between modernists and fundamentalists. It is a tragic tale. Unfortunately, as liberalism/modernism went to one extreme, evangelism went to another.

Evangelism gone sour. Since my bias is obviously pro-evangelist I take the risk of overstating this next point in the opposite direction.

Can evangelism go sour? In a sense it can and did. Listen to the reaction of evangelism to the changing scene. Much of evangelism became too one-sided in its response to modernism. Personal was pitted against social. Much of the message was guilt-ridden and filled with harangue.

Holiness theology, toward the end of the nineteenth century, became defensive and ingrown. Between 1892 and 1907 the holiness movement split twenty-five different ways. Evangelicals reacting to an onslaught of liberalism/modernism abandoned the ethical/social in favor of a "gospel" that was purely personal/experiential. Although Jonathan Edwards said that revival was a miracle—the movement of the Spirit, revivalism insisted that revival was experience-centered religion—dependent largely upon the effectiveness of the evangelist. To risk a caricature, let's take Billy Sunday (1862-1935) as an example of a style of revivalism that in many ways missed its mark. Frequently, evangelicals in the style of Billy Sunday's vaudeville antics became anti-intellectual in the face of the sophistication of theological modernism. Although evangelists like Sunday were effective in a way, their effect upon the church was minimal. They failed to stem the tide of secularism. They failed to defeat the heresies of modernism. They actually undermined the influence of the clergy. In effect, at the turn of the century, evangelism and evangelists lost the respect of most of the American people. For the next two generations evangelical revivals that were once a vital part of the life of the church became perfunctory. The evangelist became a spiritual masseur employed only once a year to tone up the body. They widened the gap between faith and works, law and gospel, between the works of the law and grace.

By and large the mentality of the Scopes "Monkey Trial" ruled the day. William Jennings Bryan was on one side and Clarence Darrow on the other. Surely the issues at stake are more important than a theory of creation. Of course the Bible is precious. It is the only absolute truth. Evangelism relies solely upon its authority. The gospel message, however, is not conveyed by the exact description of creation on the one end or the heavenly vision on the other. The gospel message is in Jesus Christ whose story is told accurately and precisely as to whom we must believe and as to how such faith moves us toward God, ourselves, and those around us. That is both personal and social. We cannot afford to choose one side of the coin. We take the one, we take the whole. That is the genius of balance. Fortunately, our tragic story is about to experience a change for the better.

Evangelism catches up. Lawrence Lacour tells a fascinating story. Just before graduating from Drew Theological Seminary, his bishop, J. Ralph Magee, visited the campus. When Lacour was asked what kind of an appointment he wanted, he quickly replied, "I would like to be appointed conference evangelist." The bishop looked somewhat surprised, but then responded, "Okay, I will appoint you, but I hope that you realize what you are getting into." When Lacour asked for clarification the bishop made an interesting comment: "When a man is ineffective in the local church or if we 'have something on him' but not enough to press charges, we appoint him conference evangelist. Are you willing to live with that kind of an image?" Lacour's response: "That doesn't bother me. God called me to be an evangelist and as a member of the Iowa Annual Conference, what better way to fulfill that calling than as conference evangelist." Lacour not only answered God's call, he changed that image. He held that position for seventeen years and served that appointment with such distinction that he went from there to become an associate secretary with the Board of Evangelism in Nashville.

Stanley Jones and Larry Lacour were not alone in reestablishing the role and influence of the evangelist in the movement called Methodism. Others such as Harry Denman and Alan Walker have made a powerful impact on the church at large. We have mentioned the role of women. Today the evangelists are not just combatting sexism, but women themselves are becoming evangelists, powerful evangelists. Let's test this last statement.

Most of us know of Aimee Semple McPherson, Kathryn Kuhlman, and Corrie ten Boom, but what of Geraldine Conway and Leontine Kelly? I have heard both of them preach with authority and power. United Methodism, like never before, is open to women evangelists. In fact, there are more women than men in some United Methodist seminaries. Women in ministry are here—I think none too soon.

The evangelist comes of age. Today, the approach of the evangelist is attempting to achieve balance without compromise. Although evangelism is not social action, social action is an evangelistic concern. The General Assembly of the United Presbyterian Church in the U.S.A., 1967, made this interesting statement:

All evangelism is mission but all mission is not necessarily evangelism. Christians often are engaged in the mission of the church without any explicit or self-conscious verbal reference to their being Christian or to the teachings of Christ. They simply allow their

113

Christ-formed consciences and concerns to cooperate with, and to take part with, other men, whether Christians, Jews, humanists, or atheists, in working for the welfare of other men. This is as it should be. God is glorified and his mercy made evident wherever and whenever men are helped to stand erect and attain the fullness of their humanity. But while this is mission it is not necessarily evangelism, and the church is constrained by the gospel to be engaged in both. To say that mission is evangelism is an inadequate equation, let alone explanation, of the Church's necessity to bring men to a time and place where they confess what the Church has been demonstrating—that Jesus is, indeed, the Lord and Saviour.

The evangelist come of age is not only well balanced, but is usually well prepared and an effective communicator. The power to change lives within comes from on high. Need I remind you that none of us, of our own persuasion, can convince red-blooded Americans to stop loving sin and start loving God. That is the work of the Holy Spirit honoring the Word that we dare to proclaim boldly.

Theologically, the evangelist is far more sophisticated than at the turn of the century. Several have Ph.D.'s and can address the world on almost any issue in light of the gospel.

The call of an evangelist today is as important as in any era of the church's history. After an age of secularism, materialism, and rationalism, many people are once again ready to reach out beyond the confines of height, width, depth, time, and motion in a willingness to trust God beyond sight. More and more the right brain is in. The left brain is out. This means that people are vulnerable to a kind of spirituality that is real. The evangelist come of age can be more real, more honest, more open and free than ever before. While freedom carries with it an added responsibility, it also opens the doors for the church that is willing to move out in faith. The evangelist must lead the way. Time is too short. Life is too precious to waste a moment. Listen to these words from Karl Barth:

The life of the one holy universal Church is determined by the fact that it is the fulfillment of the service as ambassador enjoined upon it.

Where the life of the Church is exhausted in self-serving, it smacks of death; the decisive thing has been forgotten, that this whole world is lived only in the exercise of what we called the Church's service as

114

ambassador, proclamation, *kerygma*. A Church that recognizes its commission will neither desire nor be able to petrify in any of its functions, to be the Church for its own sake. There is the "Christ-believing group"; but this group is sent out: "Go and preach the Gospel!" It does not say, "Go and celebrate services!" "Go and edify yourselves with the sermon!" "Go and celebrate the Sacraments!" "Go and present yourselves in a liturgy, which perhaps repeats the heavenly liturgy!" "Go and devise a theology which may gloriously unfold like the *Summa* of St. Thomas!" Of course, there is nothing to forbid all this; there may exist very good cause to do it all; but nothing, nothing at all for its own sake! In it all the one thing must prevail: "Proclaim the Gospel to every creature!" The Church runs like a herald to deliver the message. It is not a snail that carries its little house on its back and is so well off in it, that only now and then it sticks out its feelers, and then thinks that the "claim of publicity" has been satisfied. No, the Church lives by its commission as herald, it is *la compagnie de Dieu*. Where the Church is living, it must ask itself whether it is serving this commission or whether it is a purpose in itself? If the second is the case, then as a rule it begins to smack of the "sacred," to affect piety, to play the priest and to mumble. Anyone with a keen nose will smell it and find it dreadful! Christianity is not "sacred"; rather there breathes in it the fresh air of the Spirit. Otherwise it is not Christianity. For it is an out-and-out "wordly" thing open to all humanity: "Go into all the world and proclaim the Gospel to every creature." [3]

The relevance for today. The key word for today must be *balance*. Call it radical balance, call it uncompromising, but call it balance. A biblical approach to faith in Jesus Christ focuses both on the personal and the social. Although more will be said about this aspect of Christianity and evangelism in the chapter following, at least some comment is appropriate here. Again, although evangelism is not social justice per se, conversion to Jesus Christ provides the only impetus whereby social justice can effect lasting change. Too much of modernism found its bankruptcy in its self-sufficiency. The refusal to trust God beyond sight is to be left to one's own devices.

Although evangelism, like too much of the theology in the early part of this century, became too easily intimidated and ran for cover, today both extremes have matured greatly. Just as Karl Barth's *Church Dogmatics* put God back on the throne of grace, realizing that theology begins in God and not within ourselves, so the evangelist realized that power without purpose becomes ghost and corpse. I am proud of my evangelist brothers and sisters. Together we look forward to a marvelous future. It is just around the corner. No! It is already here.

Chapter 12: The Future

Where there is no vision, the people perish.

Proverbs 29:18(KJV)

Until now I have, for the most part, asked others to speak for me. Now it is my turn as an evangelist to speak for myself concerning the future. In so doing I want to be humble, but not too humble. Although I claim no prophetic gift, I know that I have something important to say, to the church in general, and to the evangelist in particular. I pray with all that is within me that these few lines will be worthy of such a task and that someone will find them helpful.

The future demands a vision. My wife and I just returned from Japan. In Japan the quality of Christianity is remarkable. We were deeply impressed and learned a great deal. The level of commitment to Christ and church is high and the dedication to Christian lifestyle is solid. In many ways the Japanese church sets an example for the world to follow. Yet, less than 1 percent of the Japanese people are Christian. Most are Buddhist and/or Shinto. Even more surprising is that the predominant growing "religion" of Japan seems to be high technology with materialism not far behind. The Japanese have an unusual ability to take a Western idea, copy it, and then improve on it. Japanese Christian theologians are sensitive to this "aping syndrome" among technologists and are determined not to follow suit. There is a saying in Japan that theology is created in Germany, corrected in Scotland, corrupted in America, and copied in Japan. That is offensive both to me and to them. Understandably, they want Christianity to be relevant to the Asian. Kosuke Koyama's *Waterbuffalo Theology* is an honest attempt at an Asian theology. Using terms and images familiar to the Asian farmer, he seeks to communicate the gospel within an oriental context. While I applaud the intent, several things concern me. Jesus Christ is neither East nor West. I am reminded of an American effort to Westernize Christianity. It was called the "death of God" theology. I am afraid that any concerted effort simply to Asianize Christianity will be closer to Sun Myung Moon than Jesus Christ. The answer is not in the East or West. It is in Jesus Christ.

117

While in Japan I was told that many American theologians no longer come to Japan to speak of Christ, but to learn about Eastern religions. When I lectured and preached, I spoke of Christ. I recall that the reaction at one point was polite interest. I had obviously struck a nerve. At a luncheon with a faculty of seminary professors following one of my lectures, one professor pressed me concerning my comments on the uniqueness of Christ. I responded that I believed that Christ is the answer to everyone's deepest need. Admittedly that does not mean that I am right and that 99 percent of the Japanese people are wrong. It simply means that we cannot both be right. We may both be wrong, but we cannot both be right. Furthermore, although truth never changes to accommodate what I believe truth to be, I believe that I am right, and my understanding of the biblical mandate is what motivates me. I said, further, that if Christians would speak of Christ and bear witness to the life available in him, then Japan, or the U.S., or any other nation, might experience growth among Christians. His reply: "Oh, you mean evangelism. That is only numbers." My wife and I replied together: "No! Evangelism is *people* being won to a saving knowledge of Jesus Christ." He must have gotten the point because his reaction was mild surprise that we could still speak of a vision for evangelism. People without a vision perish. Surely the answer for the future is believing God for the harvest.

The church today faces grave challenges. We could well be on the brink of a Pentecost or a holocaust. Either way God is in control. If, however, the church is to experience revival in our time, we will have to realize that God has chosen to act through the church and its obedience to the divine will. God is ready . . . already at work . . . preparing the way. The Spirit is moving preveniently in everyone the world over. Are we sensitive to God's leading? Are we expectant? Do we evangelize, looking for a response? Are we harvesters looking for the harvest?

The disciples in John 4 have just returned to the well with food. Jesus responds: "How can you think of food when the fields are ripe unto harvest?" Looking beyond the food, he was looking to the fields teeming with people coming to see for themselves if what the woman said was true. "Can this be the Christ?" (v. 29). He was, and they believed for themselves. Again, people without a vision perish. Where is the vision for evangelism today? I have seen it in Africa. Two years ago my son and I went to Kenya where we saw God at work among a people with a vision. As I preached, people responded. Why? Because those who brought them came expecting God to move, and that is precisely what happened. Recently a United Methodist lay woman from Liberia visited several churches in the U.S. She is a trained psychiatric nurse but she is also an evangelist. An article in the *United Methodist Reporter* made this comment:

Ms. [Ida Beatrice] Brooks described the booming African cities as offering lots of room for church growth. She attributed the phenomenal growth of African churches [10 percent a year] to the sense of personal responsibility held by Christians there. [She commented further:] "It has become part of our Christian tradition to share the gospel of Jesus Christ with people we meet everyday. It is quite common to see a Christian on a city bus walk over to a stranger and say, 'I found something wonderful and I want to share it with you.' We don't care who is watching us. We just want to profess publicly that we are Christians."[1]

Now that is vision! It would serve both East and West right if the answer came from Africa. Of course it will not—it will come from God through the Word. East, West, and in between need a vision that is truly biblical.

Thus far we have spoken of the future in terms of vision. The evangelists of the future must have vision enough to believe that God is not only in the message but preparing the hearts of people to receive. People with a vision are bold. The term *holy boldness* is a good term for the future. I have never stepped out on faith and regretted it. Sometimes my own preconceptions of what I really wanted or needed were misdirected but I was always better for having placed my trust in God and the Word.

The future demands an emphasis upon the Word. No one discovers God as if He were a thing discoverable by toil and instinct. God is known for one reason. He has revealed himself supremely in Jesus Christ and He has spoken the truth of that revelation clearly through a book. John Wesley writes in the preface to his *Forty-four Sermons*: "Oh give me that book! At any price, give me the book of God! I have it: here is knowledge enough for me. Let me be *homo unius libri* (a man of one book). Here then am I, far from the busy ways of men. I sit down alone: only God is here. In His presence I open, I read His book; for this end, to find the way to heaven."[2]

For evangelists the Bible is the primary source for preaching. It is our most important tool for evangelism. All things necessary for salvation are contained therein. "The word of God is living and active. Sharper than any double-edged sword, it penetrates even to dividing soul and spirit, joints and marrow; it judges the thoughts and attitudes of the heart" (Heb. 4:12). The Bible establishes doctrine and moral teaching. It speaks clearly and to the point. There is no fine print. God reveals; God does not conceal. So the Word alone is the *terminus a quo*, the starting place. To start anywhere else is to betray our method. Let me explain further.

There are basically two schools of thought as to how we come to a saving knowledge of God. Either we begin with what God has chosen to reveal "supernaturally" or we begin by finding our source somewhere within ourselves. Can we come to a saving knowledge of God apart from God's revelation? I think not. Many theologians apparently believe that original sin (if there is such a thing) corrupts only from the neck down. That is, our minds are left free first to understand God, and then to reason with our hearts, maneuvering them, as it were, to the point of faith. Again, I think not. The whole Cartesian approach (after Descartes' "I think, therefore I am") is a rope of sand. Wesley put it bluntly: "Man left to himself, will reason his way to hell." God's grace must supersede the mind as well as the heart. God alone plays the principal role in the drama of rescue. This point is so important. Let me state it still differently.

In our last chapter we mentioned Adolf von Harnack and Johann Herrmann as the epitome of liberalism. Karl Karth (1886–1968), their most noted student, reacted strongly against their liberalism along these epistomological lines. As a pastor in the Swiss town of Safenwil, Barth realized that the reductionism of the one and the subjective individualism of the other were allowing too much ministry to slip through the cracks. There had to be more to Christianity than moral principle or even social justice (although Barth was strong on both). He was simply not meeting his people's needs. They needed something from on high. They needed a word from God beyond the well-intended platitudes of their faithful pastor.

Barth became a serious student of the Bible. While I do not agree entirely with his view of inspiration, listen to these conclusions which are taken from his *Commentary on Romans*. God is beyond the reach of fallen humankind. The search for a "natural theology" is futile. God, to be known, must be revealed as Word through the scriptures or through preaching or by means of the Holy Spirit. *Humankind is more known than knowing.*

For Barth the Word has a threefold form—preached, written, and revealed. Barth's translator, Geoffrey Bromiley, summarizes this three-fold form:

The Word preached is real proclamation on the presupposition that God's Word is the commission, the theme, the judgment, and the event. The Word written implies that proclamation rests on the Word already spoken by the prophets and apostles as a given factor, that is, the canon, by which the church is called, empowered, and guided. The word revealed is the revelation which scripture recollects as written, and proclamation points forward to as promise. "In revelation our concern is with the coming Jesus Christ, God's own Word spoken by God Himself."[3]

Barth's emphasis is on the Word as the object of faith. His theology is church-related. Theology is church talk about God and is best done by pastors and teachers, not ivory tower theologians. In his *Church Dogmatics* Barth states under a section entitled the "knowability of God" that God wants to be known and is ready to be known, but cannot really be known in nature. God alone knows Himself so that He alone can reveal Himself. God reveals Himself as truth through grace. If He is to be known as lord, creator, reconciler, and redeemer, then He alone can create the analogy whereby He can be known. God, therefore, enables our readiness. We must have grace to know. We must, therefore, be open to that grace. Finally, however much we can know, Jesus Christ is the extent and limit.[4] Deism made theology totally other. German liberalism made God accessible by human resources. Barth made God again totally other but God chooses to be revealed through the Word.

Earlier I mentioned the word *Cartesian*. Let me explain and contrast that term before moving on to another heading. The real issue as suggested in the beginning is not modernism versus fundamentalism, it is Cartesian versus non-Cartesian. In other words, where do we start? Helmut Thielicke's *The Evangelical Faith* states the case clearly.[5] Cartesian theology focuses on the act of appropriation. The dominant interest is not in the message (the revealed Word) but in the hearer—humankind reaches up. It begins with anthropology. The Cartesian asks: "What point of contact does the message find in my existing conceptions?" To be relevant (so says the Cartesian) the message must accommodate itself to *me*. I have come of age. I am autonomous. The question is: How can I understand and appropriate the message so that it is my responsibility? This Cartesian approach is a shift to human-kind-centeredness. Theology is reduced to a mere chapter in anthropology. Although the Cartesian emphasis upon actualization and contemporary statement is well meaning, it results in a tragic entanglement—autonomy rules message. Any theology which builds *inductively* out of human resource to a so-called knowledge of God destroys all that transcends. It bypasses the given—the Word. In our scramble to ascend by human subjectivity, we miss that divine objectivity which has already come down.

Although the non-Cartesian approach does not deny the need for actualization and a dogmatic restatement of faith in light of modern issues (truth transported into new terms), it does not begin with the hearer. It begins with the message—the Word. It works *deductively* from that which has been revealed. God reaches down. It is the prodigal revisited. Sonship is restored only by the Father's act. Appropriation is important for the non-Cartesian, but the Word of God itself sets up the conditions. Again, the evangelists of the future must hold to the primacy of the Word. The Word discloses itself and creates its own hearers. This is done by the Holy Spirit. At this point let me continue this line of thought under a new heading.

The future demands a clear understanding of the person and work of the Holy Spirit. Closely linked with vision and an emphasis upon the Word is the person and work of the Holy Spirit. Prior to the Charismatic movement, too many mainline denominational people were leaving their mainline churches for Pentecostal churches in order to experience the fullness of God's Holy Spirit. There were several reasons for this. One was that there was simply not enough teaching on the Holy Spirit. Twenty years ago Stanley Jones was indeed ahead of his time. Now there is almost too much. Nevertheless, as evangelists we cannot afford to say too much by saying too little where the person and work of the Holy Spirit are concerned. People are hearing so much about the Holy Spirit that they come with itching ears, prepared to hear what they want to hear unless we speak clearly and to the point. Let me illustrate with the Cartesian and non-Cartesian approaches to God.

Cartesian theology finds identity in self-understanding. The ongoing self is the primary theme. This reveals itself in the many self-help approaches to life on the market today. Non-Cartesian theology finds identity in the new creation, and the whence of this new creation/identity is the primary theme. What (or perhaps more appropriately whom) is the whence of this new creation/identity? You guessed it—the Holy Spirit. By the Holy Spirit I am in Christ. As faith (itself a gift of the Spirit) looks to Jesus Christ, the Holy Spirit lays hold of me in the form of faith. Flesh as an orientation of life is no longer possible. The Spirit re-orients us. God alone moves us from old to new. But what does this mean?

The evangelists of the future must understand the work of the Spirit so that faith is not quenched but enlivened and channeled into productive ministry. Let me list just a few important themes where the person and work of the Holy Spirit are concerned.

Have we gotten the Holy Spirit into our ministry by building upon a strong prayer base? If it is true that a saving knowledge of God comes from on high, then we had best look first to God and the Word in prayerful study and preparation. The work of the Holy Spirit in pre-evangelism is important. Prevenient grace (the work of the Spirit in the life of a potential believer between conception and conversion) is at work in everyone. Do we expect our messages to take root and grow? Preaching cannot produce faith, but it can shorten the leap so that the Holy Spirit can take over.

Do we understand and have we experienced the fruit of the Spirit as love? Recently I asked a young minister, who had just complained of an inability to communicate from the pulpit, what his first feeling was when he thought of his people as a congregation about to hear him preach. His reply: "Sinners." I then asked him what his first feeling was when he thought of his two-year-old son. His reply: "Love." I told him then that when he could see his people as he saw his son, he would be an effective preacher. Again, I am reminded of George Whitefield's words describing his feelings as he stood before the people: "I see their mortality and their hurt." Again, the great commission must be seen in light of the great commandment. The Holy Spirit teaches us that love is basic. We live to the degree that we love. Love lengthens life. Last week a friend of mine died. My, how she could love! God knows she lived for a thousand years.

What of the gifts of the Spirit? Paul writes in 1 Cor. 12:1: "Concerning spiritual gifts, brethren, I would not have you be uninformed" (NIV). The evangelists today must understand and teach about the gifts of the Spirit. If we do not, someone else will. People must somehow be encouraged to divorce gifts from spirituality. God gives gifts for one reason—to equip us for ministry within the Body.

What does the Holy Spirit teach us about Christian unity? The evangelists of the future must prepare for a spiritual climate that transcends sectarian lines and draws us into fellowship with others outside our own immediate churches or denominations.

The future demands balance between personal and social. Today extreme left and right politics are yielding to a radical center. I must admit that I like that. Again, balance without compromise seems an appropriate phrase. As evangelists we must not pit ourselves against social issues that come under the mandate of scripture. Just as the spirit needs a body, power needs a purpose. Too many Christians are becoming spiritually obese for lack of mission. I stated in my book *The Partakers* that God does not equip freight trains to pull little red wagons. Freight trains are built for freight cars and battleships for the open seas. Evangelism without social concern or social concern without evangelism becomes a ghost and a corpse. We cannot afford to forget that social action is an outgrowth of (not a reaction against) the revivalism of the nineteenth century. Timothy L. Smith's classic study entitled *Revivalism and Social Reform* tells that story in great detail. He has done the church a great service.

The future demands follow-up. During our recent stay in Japan we were told by several there that a well-known American evangelist had visited for an evangelistic crusade. His ministry fell flat with little effect upon the church. Why? There was no follow-up. Lawrence Lacour had tremendous success in Japan as an evangelist. Why? He started churches, over thirty of which are now self-supporting.

We have observed Wesley, Asbury, Otterbein, Albright, and Stanley Jones build great movements out of an ability to organize new Christians into fellowships for growth and nurture. The class meetings, the *Collegia Pietatis*, and the Ashrams all served the same purpose. Something was left behind after the evangelists had spoken. If given the right kind of direction, lay Christians will hold each other accountable for spiritual formation.

Today growth groups are developing already in many churches. All the evangelist need do is underscore existing ministry. This *direct link* to the local church is vital. Whenever I go into a church for a mission I ask well in advance what is going on already. The evangelist who simply brings in new ideas, dumps them, and takes the first plane out of town is doomed to fail in having any lasting effect upon the ongoing life of the church. The evangelist who gets people in touch with their own gifts for ministry and then directs these people to opportunities for fellowship and service leaves something behind. When the evangelists leave, ministry must not go with them; ministry must stay behind.

The point about underscoring existing ministry needs one final comment. To underscore existing ministry affirms both the local pastor and the people. This creates a mutual support which is key. Then and only then is follow-up assured.

The future demands anticipation. The New Testament exhorts us to be wise in the ways of unrighteous mammon (Luke 16:9). Even in a recession some people are out there making a financial killing. They do so by anticipating the trends of the future. As Christians, we too must anticipate future trends. Admittedly, the Christian rarely listens carefully to the so-called secular prophets. They draw not so much as a ho-hum. Yet, people like Toffler (*Future Shock*), Reich (*The Greening of America*), and Naisbitt (*Megatrends*) can teach us something. True, their bark is usually bigger than their bite, but if we do not know where people are headed we could be left whistling in the dark. Let me take the latest of the books listed above (*Megatrends*) and suggest one or two future trends that might be important for the evangelist to consider.

The most obvious future trend for me relates to proliferation. People are now looking for more specific issues and answers. Naisbitt calls our attention to party politics moving to issue politics. America, once a giant melting pot, now celebrates its cultural diversity. People no longer want either/or; they want multiple options that speak more specifically to specific needs. Naisbitt, like Stanley Jones, asked: "What business are we in?" He illustrates with Mary Parker Follett who in 1904 became the first management consultant in America. She asked that same question. One of her clients was a window shade company. She moved them into "light control" and their opportunities expanded enormously.

Specificity gives a strategic vision an image—a "goal picture." John F. Kennedy did not aim for the best space program. He aimed for a man on the moon within a decade. Now that paints a picture. So, how does this one trend relate to the evangelist?

There can be little doubt that growing churches in America are meeting specific needs. They claim that God wants to meet this particular need, to heal this particular disease. Is that manipulating God? Before answering too hastily, look at the ministry of Jesus. Words such as *fish*, and *wine*, and *leprosy*, and *blindness*, come immediately to mind. Growing churches are naming the sins and diseases, the problems of life, and are calling them out. That is where the crowds are. It is no longer a decision simply between heaven and hell, but for conversion, rededication, or overcoming some specific sin such as resentment, alcoholism, or a lack of forgiveness.

Do we have enough faith to be specific again? Too long we have hidden behind the excuse of manipulating God. God cannot be manipulated! We pray and minister, seeking the mind of Christ, but if we are bold we will name the specific need and trust God to supply according to his Word.

People can visualize goal pictures. The old slogan "The world for Christ in our generation" is too broad. How about individual goals with specific time lines—will you, Jane or Mary or John, win one person for Jesus Christ this month?

Proliferation means that denominations had best allow for freedom in different kinds of worship services, else we will lose too many of our members to independent churches that do. Vatican II allowed the mass to be spoken in the native tongue of the worshiper and might well have kept Rome from serious losses. Standard revivals need a fresh look. The gospel is the same but the words to communicate it are changing.

Finally, women have come a long way (not that they have yet reached their full potential). In the 1950s there were fewer than 100,000 new companies started per year. Today, 600,000 companies are started per year and one-third by women. The shift in America is not just from industrial to informational, it is male to female in many areas. The church is following suit. The America of the future might well be white collar and female. The admonition in 1 Peter might prove more and more prophetic: "Husbands, in the same way be considerate as you live with your wives, and treat them with respect as the weaker partner and as heirs with you of the gracious gift of life, so that nothing will hinder your prayers" (NIV). If this offends, just one final comment. Weakness in the New Testament is not so much something to be overcome, it is the place where God dwells. Think about it.

The relevance for today. Is this still necessary in a chapter on the future? You bet. Anticipating the future is just as relevant for today as studying the past. Besides, it gives us an opportunity to give a brief review.

Ministry must have a vision! Faith is the conviction of things not seen. God would have us dreaming.

Ministry focuses on the Word. Jesus Christ is God's supreme revelation as Word incarnate. Is the evangelist still needed? More people today are without a gospel witness than ever before. Evangelism looks to the Holy Spirit. Our listeners today place greater demands upon us as to how the Spirit works and what we as Christians have a right to expect as the result of our faith in Jesus Christ.

Conversion is not an isolated experience. It is for service. The balance between personal and social is essential for a vital Christian witness.

Future trends do not establish our agenda. That has already been established by God. Future trends describe the vehicle upon which the gospel is carried.

Our study has introduced many evangelists who in their own way and in their own time anticipated the future. They trusted God and acted according to the Word. They give us giant shoulders upon which to stand as we look to the future. Ultimately, however, although we stand on these human shoulders, the giant shoulders upon which we build our evangelism belong only to one—Jesus Christ. To him be the glory forever and ever. Amen.

NOTES

Chapter 1

1. *Journal*, Curnock ed., Volume I, p. 442.
2. Ibid., p. 448.
3. *Works*, Jackson ed., Volume V, pp. 8 f.
4. Ibid., pp. 60 f.
5. Ibid., p. 61.
6. *Works*, Volume I, p. 100.
7. Ibid., p. 102.
8. *Works*, Volume V, p. 61.
9. John Whitehead, *The Life of John Wesley*, Volume II, pp. 463 ff (London, 1796), and Robert Southey, *The Life of John Wesley*, Volume II, pp. 338 ff (New York, 1855).
10. Southey, *Life*, Volume II, p. 340.
11. Ibid., p. 343.
12. Whitehead, *Life*, Volume II, p. 469.
13. *Works*, Volume VIII, pp. 343 f.
14. Whitehead, *Life*, Volume II, pp. 466 f.
15. *Works*, Volume VIII, p. 272.
16. Whitehead, *Life*, Volume II, p. 467.
17. Ibid., p. 478.
18. *Works*, Volume VIII, p. 341.
19. Ibid., p. 343.

Chapter 2

1. There are conflicting reports as to who the first lay preacher (or evangelist) was. One source names a Mr. Bowers, another Joseph Humphreys (a Moravian). The confusion lies in the fact that neither Bowers nor Humphreys was out of the Methodist connection. We know with a fair amount of certainty that Thomas Maxfield was the first of the Methodist Society to serve as a lay preacher. Cf. Southey, *Life of Wesley*, Vol. I, p. 332 and Wesley's *Journal*, Vol. VIII, p. 93.
2. Maxfield later left the Methodists.
3. Throughout this chapter, the terms *preacher* and *evangelist* are used synonymously, since by Wesley's definition they are interchangeable.
4. Southey, *Life*, Vol. I, p. 333.
5. Ibid., p. 334.
6. Ibid.
7. The relationship between the lay preacher/evangelist and minister will be developed at some length in chapter 3. Cf. for the moment the sermon "The Ministerial Office" (*Works*, Vol. VII, pp. 273ff.) where Wesley insists that evangelists are not pastors."
8. *Works*, Vol. XIII, p. 219.
9. *Lives of the Early Methodist Preachers*, Jackson ed., London, 1872, Vol. IV, pp. 22ff.

10. Ibid., p. 24.
11. *Letters*, Telford ed., Vol. IV, p. 33.
12. Whitehead, *Life*, Vol. II, p. 336.
13. Ibid.
14. *Letters*, Vol. III, p. 100.
15. *Lives*, Vol. II, p. 86.
16. *Lives*, Vol. IV, p. 38.
17. Whitehead, *Life*, Vol. II, p. 322.
18. Ibid., p. 337.
19. *Works*, New Oxford ed., Vol. XV, p. 217.
20. Whitehead, *Life*, Vol. II, p. 204.
21. Ibid., p. 322.
22. *Letters*, Vol. IV, p. 133.
23. *Letters*, Vol. IV, p. 164; Vol. V, p. 257.
24. *Letters*, Vol. V, p. 302.
25. Ibid., p. 305.
26. *Letters*, Vol. VIII, p. 101f.
27. *Letters*, Vol. VI, pp. 85; 93.
28. *Journal*, Vol. VI, p. 338.
29. *Wesley Historical Society Proceedings*, Vol. VI, p. 45.
30. *Works*, Vol. VII, pp. 125f.
31. *Letters*, Vol. VI, p. 272.
32. *Works*, Vol. VII, p. 277.

Chapter 3

1. *Works*, Vol. XIII, p. 219.
2. *Works*, Vol. VII, p. 275. Henry Moore's *Life of Wesley* takes issue with Wesley on this matter. In fact Moore records a personal conversation that he had with Wesley: " 'Sir, you know that the *Evangelists* Timothy and Titus were ordered by the apostle to ordain *Bishops* in every place; and surely they could not impart to them an authority which they did not themselves possess.' He [Mr. Wesley] looked earnestly at me for some time, but not with displeasure. He made no reply and soon introduced another subject. I said no more. The man of *one book* would not dispute against it. I believe he saw his love to the Church, from which he never deviated unnecessarily had, in this instance, led him a little too far" (Henry Moore, *Life*, Vol. II, p. 339).
3. *Works*, Vol. VII, pp. 427 f.
4. Colin Williams, in his book *John Wesley's Theology Today*, has an appendix (pp. 207-42) which speaks directly to John Wesley's views on separation.
5. *Proceedings of the Wesley Historical Society*, Vol. XXVII, pp. 715 f.
6. Davies and Rupp, *A History of the Methodist Church in Great Britain*, Vol. I, p. 231.
7. *Journal*, Vol. III, p. 232. The full title of Lord King's work is *An Inquiry into the Constitution, Discipline, Unity, and Worship of the Primitive Church* (London, 1691).
8. *Letters*, Vol. III, pp. 135, 182; Vol. IV, p. 150; Vol. VII, pp. 20-21.
9. Davies and Rupp, *A History of the Methodist Church in Great Britain*, Vol. I, p. 246.
10. *Letters*, Vol. VII, pp. 30-31.
11. Davies and Rupp, *A History of the Methodist Church in Great Britain*, Vol. II, p. 147.
12. *Letters*, Vol. VII, p. 262.

13. Ibid., p. 238.
14. *Proceedings of the Wesley Historical Society*, Vol. IX, p. 151.
15. Asbury makes an interesting defense of Wesley's ordinations (Asbury's *Letters*, III, pp. 548 f) in light of Whitehead's strong opposition (Whitehead's *Life*, II, pp. 418-38).
16. *Proceedings of the Wesley Historical Society*, Vol. IX, p. 152.
17. Ibid., pp. 149 ff. An article entitled "Wesley's Ordinations."
18. John Vickers, *Thomas Coke* (Abingdon, 1969), p. 199.
19. Davies and Rupp, *A History of the Methodist Church in Great Britain*, Vol. II, p. 153.
20. Ibid. In 1836 the Certificate of Ordination read: "Ordination or Admission into Full-Connection."

Chapter 4

1. *Minutes of the Annual Conference of the Methodist Episcopal Church 1773-1828* (New York: Mason and Lane, 1840), pp. 7; 17-18.
2. Francis Asbury, *Journal and Letters* (Abingdon, 1958), Vol. I, pp. 720 ff.
3. Ibid., p. 721.
4. The only published works by Asbury other than his *Journals and Letters* (3 volumes) are a few extracts from Jeremiah Burroughs and Richard Baxter, some extracts from letters by preachers and members of the Methodist Episcopal Church, and a selection of hymns to supplement the *Methodist Pocket Hymn-Book*.
5. *Journal and Letters*, Vol. I, p. 116.
6. *Journal and Letters*, Vol. I, p. 682; cf. *Journal and Letters*, Vol. I, p. 766, for an outline on 2 Chron. 15:2, and Vol. I, p. 756, for an outline on Hebrews 6:4-8, two of his favorite texts.
7. Ibid., p. 744.
8. Ibid., p. 164.
9. Ibid., p. 133.
10. Ibid., p. 323.
11. Ibid.
12. Ibid., p. 285.
13. Ibid., p. 126.
14. Ibid., p. 678.
15. Ibid., p. 5.
16. Ibid., p. 420.
17. Ibid., p. 299; cf. p. 421.
18. Ibid., pp. 481 f.
19. Ibid., p. 351.
20. Ibid., cf. pp. 488, 564, and 594.
21. *Journal and Letters*, Vol. II, p. 416 f.
22. *Journal and Letters*, Vol. I, p. 269.
23. Ibid., p. 264.
24. Ibid., p. 266.
25. Ibid., p. 270.
26. Ibid., p. 269.
27. Ibid., p. 323.
28. Ibid., p. 53.
29. *Journal and Letters*, Vol. II, p. 51.

30. Nathan Bangs, *A History of the Methodist Episcopal Church* (New York: Mason and Lane, 1838), Vol. II, pp. 398-399.
31. *Journal and Letters*, Vol. I, p. 351.
32. Ibid., p. 166.
33. *Journal and Letters*, Vol. III, p. 269.
34. Ibid., p. 196.
35. Ibid., p. 251; cf. 255.
36. *Journal and Letters*, Vol. I, p. 131.
37. *Journal and Letters*, Vol. II, p. 694.
38. *Journal and Letters*, Vol. I, p. 247.

Chapter 5

1. Samuel Drew, *Life of Coke* (New York, 1818), p. 64.
2. Whitehead, *Life of Wesley*, Vol. II, pp. 415 f.
3. Ibid., p. 416.
4. See *A History of the Methodist Church in Great Britain*, Vol. II, p. 149.
5. Thomas Coke, *Extracts of the Journals of the Reverend Dr. Coke's Five Visits to America* (1793), pp. 15 f.
6. Asbury's *Journals*, Vol. I, pp. 472 f.
7. Frederick Norwood, *The Story of American Methodism* (Abingdon, 1974), p. 100.
8. Quoted in Holland McTyeire, *A History of Methodism* (Nashville, 1893), p. 342.
9. *Letters*, Vol. VII, p. 239.
10. Ibid.
11. The word spelled thusly in the *Sunday Service*, but not normally elsewhere.
12. These figures vary somewhat in different accounts. No official minutes have survived.
13. McTyeire, *History of Methodism*, p. 349.
14. Ibid.
15. Ibid.
16. Ibid., pp. 352 f.
17. Ibid., pp. 350 f.
18. *Southern Quarterly Review*, July, 1885, p. 377.
19. Asbury, *Journals*, Vol. I, p. 476.
20. McTyeire, *History of Methodism*, p. 353.

Chapter 6

1. Southey, *Life of Wesley*, Vol. II, pp. 206-9.
2. Asbury, *Journal and Letters*, Vol. I, pp. 340 f. Garrettson had been jailed on February 27, 1780.
3. Nathan Bangs, *The Life of the Reverend Freeborn Garrettson: Compiled From His Printed and Manuscript Journals and Other Authentic Documents* (New York, 1829), pp. 49 f.
4. Nathan Bangs, *The Life*, p. 50.
5. Quoted in Luccock, Hutchinson, Goodloe, *The Story of Methodism* (Abingdon, 1926), p. 224.
6. Ibid., p. 230.

7. Ibid., pp. 224 f.
8. Quoted in McTyeire, *History of Methodism*, p. 424.
9. McTyeire, *History of Methodism*, pp. 420 f. For additional information see LeRoy M. Lee, *The Life and Times of the Reverend Jesse Lee* (Louisville, 1848). Jesse Lee himself also wrote a History of Methodism, which some might find interesting.
10. J. B. Wakeley, *The Heroes of Methodism*, (New York, 1856), p. 226.
11. *Proceedings of the Wesley Historical Society*, Vol. 9, p. 16.
12. *Coke's Journal* (1793), p. 18.
13. Asbury *Journal and Letters*, Vol. I, p. 362.
14. Ibid., p. 403.
15. Ibid.
16. Ibid., p. 413.
17. Herbert Asbury, *A Methodist Saint* (New York, 1727), pp. 159 f.

Chapter 7

1. Raymond Albright, *A History of the Evangelical Church* (Harrisburg, PA: The Evangelical Press, 1945), p. 46.
2. Arthur C. Core, *Philip William Otterbein: Pastor, Ecumenist* (Dayton: United Brethren Publishing House, 1968), p. 77-90. The sermon is given here in its entirety.
3. J. Bruce Behney and Paul H. Eller, *The History of the Evangelical United Brethren Church* (Abingdon, 1979), p. 36 f.
4. Arthur Core, *Otterbein*, p. 87.
5. Ibid., p. 85.
6. Ibid., p. 90.
7. Ibid., p. 91.
8. Behney and Eller, *The History of the Evangelical United Brethren Church*, p. 49.
9. A. W. Drury, *History of the Church of the United Brethren in Christ* (Dayton: United Brethren Publishing House, 1924), pp. 51-52.
10. Henry Spayth, *History of the Church of the United Brethren in Christ* (Circleville, Ohio; Conference Office of the United Brethren in Christ, 1851), p. 19.
11. H. A. Thompson, *Our Bishops* (Dayton: United Brethren Publishing House, 1904), p. 31.
12. Christian Newcomer, *Journal*, September 28, 1800, p. 74.
13. Henry Harbaugh, *The Fathers of the German Reformed Church in Europe and America* (Lancaster: J. M. Westhaeffer, 1872), Vol. II, p. 74.
14. Arthur Core, *Otterbein*, p. 29.
15. George Miller, *Leben Erfahrung and Amtsführung Zweyer Evangelischer Prediger Jacob Albrecht und Georg Miller* (Neu-Berlin, 1834), p. 12 f.
16. Behney and Eller, *The History of the Evangelical United Brethren Church*, p. 84.
17. George Miller, *Leben*, p. 14 f.
18. Behney and Eller, *The History of the Evangelical United Brethren Church*, p. 72.
19. W. W. Orwig, *History of the Evangelical Association* (Cleveland, 1858), p. 20.
20. Raymond Albright, *A History of the Evangelical Church*, p. 52.
21. Behney and Eller, *The History of the Evangelical United Brethren Church*, p. 72.
22. George Miller, *Leben*, pp. 16-18.
23. Frederick Norwood, *The Story of American Methodism* (Abingdon, 1974), p. 116.

Chapter 8

1. F. Ernest Stoeffler, *Continental Pietism and Early American Christianity* (Eerdmans, 1976), p. 216. Cf. also J. Steven O'Malley's definitive work on the Herborn influence on Otterbein entitled *Pilgrimage of Faith: The Legacy of the Otterbeins* (Metuchen, NJ: Scarecrow Press, 1973).
2. Henry G. Spayth, *History of the Church of the United Brethren in Christ*, p. 83.
3. Quoted in Core, *Otterbein*, p. 32.
4. Drury, *Disciplines of the United Brethren in Christ*, 1814-1841, p. 10.
5. Henry Boehm, "Manuscript of the Journal of Henry Boehm" microfilm, United Methodist Archives, pp. 120-121.
6. Miller composed the first Evangelical Association *Discipline* after Albright's death as well as the devotional classic *Practical Christianity* and the first biography of Jacob Albright.
7. Quoted in Behney and Eller, *The History of the Evangelical United Brethren Church*, p. 75.
8. O'Malley has written a manuscript entitled *Touched by Godliness: John Seybert and the United Methodist Heritage* (as yet unpublished).
9. Raymond Albright, *The History of the Evangelical Church*, p. 260.
10. Samuel P. Spreng, *The Life and Labors of John Seybert* (Cleveland, Ohio, 1888), pp. 369 f.
11. Behney and Eller, *The History of the EUB Church*, p. 221.
12. Raymond Albright, *A History of the Evangelical Church*, pp. 17 f.

Chapter 9

1. Steve O'Malley, *Pilgrimage of Faith* (Metuchen, NJ: The Scarecrow Press, Inc., 1973), pp. 189 f.
2. Raymond Albright, *A History of the Evangelical Church* (The Evangelical Press, 1945), p. 261.
3. Cf. Albright, *A History of the Evangelical Church*, pp. 359 f. and Behney and Eller, *The History of the Evangelical United Brethren Church*, pp. 247 f.
4. Albright, *A History of the Evangelical Church*, p. 360.
5. George Miller, *Leben*, pp. 15 f.
6. Albright, *A History of the Evangelical Church*, p. 262. Cf. O'Malley's yet unpublished manuscript entitled: *Touched by Godliness: John Seybert and the United Methodist Heritage*.
7. John Wesley, *Letters* (Pelford Edition), Vol. IV, p. 103.
8. P. Hackenberg, *A Short Review of the Most Important Teachings of the Christian Religion* (New Berlin, 1838), p. 6.
9. *The Evangelical Messenger*, 1848, Vol. I, numbers 4 and 5.

Chapter 10

1. E. Stanley Jones, *A Song of Ascents* (Abingdon Press, 1968), p. 28.
2. Quoted in *A Song of Ascents*, p. 92.
3. E. Stanley Jones, *A Song of Ascents*, p. 99.

4. Ibid., p. 44.
5. Ibid., p. 309.
6. Ibid., p. 53.
7. Ibid., p. 57.
8. E. Stanley Jones, *Victorious Living* (Abingdon, 1936), p. 79.
9. E. Stanley Jones, *The Christ of the American Road* (Abingdon, 1944), p. 7.
10. E. Stanley Jones, *A Song of Ascents*, p. 53.
11. Ibid., p. 109.
12. Ibid., p. 102.
13. Ibid., p. 42
14. Ibid., pp. 274 f.
15. Ibid., pp. 273 f.
16. Ibid., p. 80.
17. *Chicago Daily News*, January 11, 1964.
18. E. Stanley Jones, *Christian Maturity*, p. 43.

Chapter 11

1. William G. McLoughlin, Jr., *Modern Revivalism* (The Ronald Press, 1959), pp. 158 f.
2. Ibid., p. 159.
3. Karl Barth, *Church Dogmatics* (T and T Clark, 1961), p. 127.

Chapter 12

1. *United Methodist Reporter*, May 6, 1983.
2. John Wesley, *Forty-four Sermons* (The Epworth Press, 1944), p. vi.
3. Geoffrey Bromiley, *Historical Theology* (Eerdmans, 1978), p. 408.
4. Karl Barth, *Church Dogmatics* (T & T Clark, Edinborough, 1957), Vol. 2, part 1, pp. 9-17.
5. Helmut Thielicke, *The Evangelical Faith* (Grand Rapids, MI: Eerdmans, 1974).